HELPING PEOPLE WORK TOGETHER:
A GUIDE TO PARTICIPATIVE WORKING PRACTICES

WRITTEN AND COMPILED

BY

ROBIN DOUGLAS   **DAVID PUGH**
DOUG ETTRIDGE   **CHRIS PAYNE**
DIANA FEARNHEAD   **DAVID SOWTER**

With the help of John Morgan, Ray Hedges and other course members and tutors from the 1982 course in Management and Practice at the National Institute for Social Work.

Illustrations by Hywel Francis

Published 1988
by the National Institute for Social Work
5 Tavistock Place, London WC1

© National Institute for Social Work

Further copies of this publication are
avaiable from the National Institute for
Social Work.

ISBN 0 902 789 42 2

AUTHORS' DETAILS

Robin Douglas — Formerly Lecturer in
Management, Organisation
and Planning, NISW;
currently Fellow in
Health and Social
Services Development,
King's Fund College, London.

Doug Ettridge — Community Social Work Manager,
London Borough of
Hammersmith and Fulham

Diana Fearnhead — Project Leader, Barnardo's
Ferncliff Centre, Hackney

Chris Payne — Lecturer and Consultant in
Social Services Development,
NISW

David Pugh — Senior Social Worker,
Gloucestershire Social Services

David Sowter — Assistant Educational Officer,
Lancashire County Council.

ACKNOWLEDGEMENTS

First we must thank all the members and staff of the 1982 M.A.P. Course, who did so much of the ground work in preparation for this book.

Then a special thanks to Theresa Curtiss for bearing the brunt of the typing of the several drafts which were used by the group to make their various revisions. Also to Karen Palmer of the National Institute for Social Work for typing the final manuscript.

FOREWORD

This guide is produced by a group of people who all met and worked together on the Course in Management and Practice in the Personal Social Services at the National Institute for Social Work.

An important aim of the course was to encourage the development of participative management practices and this was reflected in the way the course was organised and in the choice of teaching methods and approaches. An important feature of this particular course was the personal choice workshops, which produced opportunities to explore the practical applications of course content and methods to individual work situations.

It was in one of the workshops that a group decided to consider the practical application of the teaching methods used on the course for day to day management and working practices.

This guide is the result of the workshop and the techniques and methods described in it have all been employed in its production too.

The basic ideas and contents were developed at the end of the course by a large workshop group which convened to discuss and identify which of the learning techniques used on the course might be applied to daily work situations. Following this workshop a smaller group decided to continue after the course with a view to producing a practical guide to participative working practices which could be used by managers and practitioners in a wide range of social services settings (fieldwork teams, day and residential settings etc) and in related human service organisations (eg. health care and education).

The group has met on several occasions over a period of three years, with individuals taking away particular sections or tasks to work on privately. The final structure and contents of the guide have taken shape gradually, being subject to much debate and revision. Having obtained agreement on the broad structure and contents, the final drafting and editing were delegated to two members of the group (Diana Fearnhead and Chris Payne). They produced a draft manuscript which was circulated to the rest of the group, whose comments and criticisms have been incorporated into this final version.

Diana Fearnhead
Chris Payne
December 1987

SUMMARY OF CONTENTS

This guide is divided into three parts. Part 1 contains discussion on the assumptions and purpose of the guide and some concepts to inform the selection of the methods and techniques that are the "meat" of the book. The third and last chapter of Part 1 offers some criteria and practical guidance for choosing and using these contents. We have deliberately tried to keep the theory to the minimum, however. The book is perhaps best seen as a kind of "cookbook" with the contents of Part 2 providing instructions on the production of particular "recipes" and those of Part 3 as samples of "set menus".

I   INTRODUCTION TO "HELPING PEOPLE WORK TOGETHER"   7

    1   The Idea of Participative Management
    2   Working in Groups
    3   Choosing and Using Methods and Techniques

II   METHODS AND TECHNIQUES (Individual Recipes)   23

    A   Setting the Agenda
    B   Effecting Introductions
    C   Making More Effective Use of Group Resources
    D   Assessing and Working on Problems
    E   Reviewing Progress and Process
    F   Taking Decisions by Voting
    G   Endings
    H   Using Audio/Visual Aids
    I   Focussing and Structuring Techniques

III   EXAMPLES OF TECHNIQUES IN ACTION (Set Menus)   91

    (a)   A Meeting Called to Obtain a Group Response to an Agency Working Party Document.
    (b)   A Day Workshop to Examine Behaviour Problems of Children in a Day Nursery.
    (c)   The Use of Sculpting Techniques by an Area Team Facing Reorganisation.
    (d)   A Day Workshop to Review the Structure of Meetings in an Area Social Services Team.

PART 1
INTRODUCTION

PART 1

INTRODUCTION TO "HELPING PEOPLE WORK TOGETHER"

CONTENTS

CHAPTER 1   THE IDEA OF PARTICIPATIVE MANAGEMENT

    a) Why Participation?   **11**

        (i)   The need to "humanise" Welfare Organisations.

        (ii)   Management is not only about what "managers" do.

        (iii) Achieving greater consistency between formal and informal work processes.

        (iv) Making better use of time.

        (v)   Involving the consumers of services.

        (vi) Continuing learning opportunities.

    b) Objections   **11**

        (i)   Participative approaches are risky.

        (ii)   Participation needs boundaries.

        (iii) Participation will inevitably show up contradictions.

        (iv) Participation needs agreement.

    c) Reviewing the working practices in your organisation.   **12**

CHAPTER 2   WORKING IN GROUPS

    a) The importance of being able to work in groups.   **13**

        (i)   The importance of the "team".

        (ii)   Working in groups is a feature of most organisations.

        (iii) Identifying and assessing membership of work groups.

    b) The need to work on different group functions.   **15**

    c) Working on "beginnings", "middles" and "endings".   **16**

        (i)   Beginnings

        (ii)   Middles — Assessing and working on problems

        (iii) Moving On.

        (iv) Endings

    d) Tasks and skills in working with groups.   **17**

        (i)   Interpersonal Skills

        (ii)   Receiving Skills

        (iii) Feedback Skills

    e) Reviewing and evaluating work groups.   **19**

CHAPTER 3   CHOOSING AND USING METHODS AND TECHNIQUES

      a)   Effective management is responsive man-   **21**
           agement.

           (i)   Taking risks

           (ii)   Managing resistances to change.

           (iii)   Involving the group in choosing and using.

           (iv)   Think carefully before choosing.

      b)   How to use the rest of the book.   **21**

           (i)   Guidelines

           (ii)   Format

           (iii)   Where to Start

CHAPTER 1

THE IDEA OF PARTICIPATIVE MANAGEMENT

The purpose of this guide is to provide some practical tools to assist people who work together in groups or "teams" to carry out their tasks efficiently and creatively. Any work group—a senior management group, a team of social workers, the staff of a hospital ward, residential or day centre—must engage continuously in planning, organising and carrying out their tasks of providing effective services. They must also engage in a variety of ways with members of other work groups inside and outside their own organisation.

Engagement in these processes involves engagement with one another, hence the emphasis we place in this book on the idea of "participation". The book represents a search for ways and means by which members of work groups can be encouraged and supported to make appropriate and effective contributions to the achivement of their goals and tasks.

a) Why participation?

In brief we would answer as follows:

(i) The need to "humanise" welfare organisations

It is our view that to be effective, human service organisations should be "human" in everything that they do. Services designed to improve the quality of people's lives should not be devised and dispensed, as it were, by a faceless and mindless machine. Organisational practices should demonstrate that the people employed to deliver services to others are themselves capable of being human in their own working lives and relationships. Attention has to be paid not only to the end product but to the processes by which services are planned and delivered. Working practices cannot be directed only to the achievement of stated goals. How work groups express themselves in their ways of working together and relationships is just as important. This is important not only from the point of view of satisfaction, but to ensure that time and energy are used creatively and effectively.

(ii) Management is not only about what "managers" do

Our approach to working practices reinforces the idea of management as a process. Management is not only about what people in managerial positions do, but the processes of planning and action have to be managed by all those in the various stages. A view of management as process implies participation. It follows that a conscious effort to think out the most effective ways of involving people in work processes must be made. This in turn will reduce the pressures, which can all too often increase to unmanageable proportions, on managers to feel solely responsible and accountable. Even if the manager is deemed accountable within the hierarchy the felt responsibilities will at least be shared. Such an approach can help diminish an unconstructive conflict of opinion between "us" and "them".

(iii) Achieving greater consistency between formal and informal work processes.

In most work organisations power is exercised and decisions taken through both formal and informal processes. The latter are particularly powerful. We have all had experiences where the key decisions have been taken outside of the established formalised decision-making structures. These experiences can leave us helpless, frustrated and powerless to influence decisions.

Genuinely participative working practices at least help to reduce the inconsistences and contradictions, often experienced between the formal and informal decision-making processes. At their best they reduce the need for secrecy and hidden agendas so that decisions can be taken openly. One other advantage is that structural changes become easier to initiate and implement as change can occur because there is a will for change. This is likely to achieve a more vibrant and responsive organisation.

(iv) Making better use of time.

Contrary to common belief, participation does not in itself inhibit or delay decision-making, neither is it necessarily inefficient in the use of time. Participation is ineffectual if unorganised or based on hazy ideas about the virtue of "being democratic". Participation, to be effective, requires the planned use of time and understanding about what are appropriate and relevant matters to be participating in. In stating this it must, however, be acknowledged that to acquire the necessary skills takes time. People have to be given time to acquire the confidence in practice which strengthens commitment and belief. They will also need to be supported when mistakes are made and crises of confidence are experienced. These often bring a temporary, if intense, desire to revert to more traditional ways of working, i.e. to being "led" or to "lead". But if people are involved in taking decisions, for example, about change, they are more likely to be committed to implementing the change being planned than if their views are ignored or suppressed. How often are ways and means found of blocking, delaying, watering down ideas, whatsoever their intrinsic merits, simply because they have been sent down from "on high" without consideration of what they will mean and imply for those who are expected to carry them out?

(v) Involving the consumers of services.

An organisation that values participation in its own working practices is more likely to apply these principles in its relationship with consumers and other agencies. Also individual members are supported and encouraged to tap consumer knowledge and experience directly and to value the results. Similar attitudes are developed in respect of inter-agency relations and a free flow of information can be enhanced. Strategies to involve consumers in planning, decision taking and direct management of activites can be developed on similar lines to approaches for involving staff.

(vi) Continuing learning opportunities.

Many of the methods and techniques described in this book are derived from adult learning principles and practices. These emphasise the use of structuring group experiences as a means of facilitating individual learning. Similarly the introduction of participative practices into the life of a work group provides opportunities for continuous learning from the exchange of ideas and experiences that are built into the process.

b) Objections

No doubt you will have heard and read about much of this before. "Fine in theory, hopeless in practice", you may be saying. "You can't change large bureaucratic machines". You may not even agree with the assumptions that are being made. "It's not our job to take decisions, that's the job of management" or " We are employed to put policies (as defined by 'them') into practice". You may even enjoy being anti-management and unprepared to accept the felt responsibilities that participation requires.

You may agree that participation is desirable, but stuck as to how it can be made to work. "Where do we begin?" "How do we get started?" "Will we be seen as subversives or as 'pie in the sky' by the rest of the organisation?" "How can we motivate those individual members of our work group who appear to be 'stuck' in their ways and are unwilling to change and try something different?"

You may also have to address genuine problems about, for example, "accountability". Who is ultimately responsible for decisions that are taken collectively? Or problems related to the fact that your organisation is structured on rather different (i.e. non-participative) assumptions. Why should the "team leader" be paid more than others if he is not going to accept a greater burden of responsibility? How will a more participative approach be viewed by the rest of your organisation, "higher" management in particular? Will it not insist that you conform to established ways of working?

In response to these and similar questions it is possible to make the following statements, which act as caveats to unbridled and uncritical enthusiasm on the one hand and as antidotes to the cynic and pessimist on the other.

(i) Participative approaches are risky.

Because the processes of arriving at decisions etc. are open and public, failures to agree or achieve results are also made public. However the opposite is also true, and the proof of the pudding will come in the eating. Successful outcomes are more likely to result in greater commitment to the organisation and its aims. There will be greater loyalty to the decisions which are taken. You are more likely to accept decisions with which you personally disagree having had the opportunity to express your point of view and having had those views genuinely taken into account than if you have not been involved at all or had them given token consideration only.

(ii) Participation needs boundaries.

In other ways it is important to cut your suit according to your cloth. It may well be that you will have to develop your participatory practices in some very modest ways, initially "testing the water" as it were within a staff meeting or working party. For more ambitious changes there will have to be a strategy to match, e.g. a range of initial planning and consultation mechanisms to ensure that commitment and appropriate methods are developed and difficulties tackled constructively.

(iii) Participation will inevitably show up contradictions.

For example, accusations of tokenism or of crypto-dictatorship are always likely to be levelled at individuals who appear to be taking a stronger lead in discussions than others. Contradictions will also appear in relationships with other parts of the organisation. However, the fact that there are contradictions should not act as a deterrent. Life is never perfect.

(iv) Participation needs agreement.

That is from those involved, and at least some recognition and passive support from people not directly involved. Imposing a participative approach can be much worse than doing nothing!

c) Reviewing the working practices in your organisation

Just look for a moment at your organisation and ask yourselves how participative are the working practices in it. For example, think of a particular management issue or piece of work and answer the following:

— Who is involved?

— Who decides how you are to work on the issues in question?

— Do senior staff usually run or chair any meetings in which this kind of issue is discussed?

— How are the decisions taken? By whom?

— Do decisions need senior management agreement before they can be implemented?

Also more generally:

— Do other members of staff share your views on participation?

— Do decisions need senior management agreement before they can be implemented?

— Does your approach fit in with the view of the rest of your organisation? Why?

An assessment of ideas in which participation already exists and the level of participation (i.e. whether genuine or tokenistic) should indicate where changes to your working practices can and should be made to increase the level of participation.

CHAPTER 2

WORKING IN GROUPS

In this second introductory chapter we discuss the role of the work group as a basic way of working for many people. This being the case it is important to develop ways and means of making groups effective and efficient by ensuring that everyone can make a full contribution.

a) The importance of being able to work in groups

It is often underestimated how much of organisational life is spent in groups. A picture of an individual on her/his own behind a desk with sporadic encounters, face-to-face or by telephone, with others working similarly does not represent accurately the realities of much of working life. Ask any group of staff, practitioners, supervisors or managers, from any human service organisation, how many work groups they belong to and you will be surprised how quickly the count runs into double figures. (See Fig 2.2).

(i) The importance of the "team"

Most people will also be able to identify at least one major grouping, which acts for them as a reference or base group. Such a group is often referred to as the "team" (although the members may not always work together). This group is often regarded as the main source of support. Opinions vary as to who should be in the "team" and membership changes over time.[1]

In a genuinely participatory approach the "team" as a whole (rather than individuals with delegated authority) can be expected to assume collectively an increasingly greater share of the responsibility for the "management" of the work, that is, in terms of the planning, preparing, implementing, reviewing and evaluating of decisions and activities and taking on a general responsibility for the shaping of the team's direction and style. (See Fig 2.1)

In team working there is one basic assumption that must be held and shared by all, namely that all activities in which individuals engage are likely to have some repercussions on others. For example an individual worker who makes a bid for resources in order to develop a personal project must realise that he/she may possibly be depriving others of resources for their projects. A decision as to a limited amount of resources has then to be taken against an agreed list of team priorities.[2] For a participatory approach to be effective the means for exchanging information, planning and co-ordinating activities, taking appropriate decisions etc., have all to be developed.

(ii) Working in groups is a feature of most organisations

Leaving aside the ideology of teamwork a more general point remains. Many workers in other hierarchial organisations spend much of their working life in groups. How they contribute to those groups can have important effects on the effectiveness and efficiency of the organisation and its capacity to deliver services. It follows that all need to develop understanding of work group processes; also skills in working in groups. They need these not only as leaders, but as participants and contributors to the achievement of agreed group goals. Some of the skills involve the use of often simple techniques to structure and focus discussions, which otherwise become "free running", lose their point and waste valuable time.

At any point in time it is possible that individuals will contribute to several work groups. Some are likely to be permanent and relatively continuous e.g. a regular staff meeting. Others may have a fixed life and are short term, e.g. a working party. Some groups meet over a long period of time, but only occasionally. Some, like staff meetings, may have a constant structure (eg. set time and procedures) but the content, membership and processes change from one session to another. Some groups will have an "open" and changing membership, eg. when a variety of views are being sought; others closed, with a permanent membership. Some groups will be at the beginning of their working life, others nearing the end or just beginning to "wind down". Some may generate considerable energy, commitment and enthusiasm; others are like a wet engine, difficult to get any spark of life in them. This book includes a variety of techniques for managing the different processes which membership of different kinds of groups entail.

(iii) Identifying and assessing membership of work groups

Fig. 2.2 provides a method for identifying and assessing the different work groups to which you belong. Having identified these ask yourself:

(i)   How many are "permanent" and meet frequently?

(ii)   How many are relatively long-term but meet only occasionally?

(iii)   Are there groups that are time-limited or relatively short-term?

(iv)   How many groups have an "open" or "changing" membership compared to those that have a permanent membership?

Would you see the need to make any changes to the structure and arrangements for any of these groups?

Fig.2.1. The Work Process of a Team

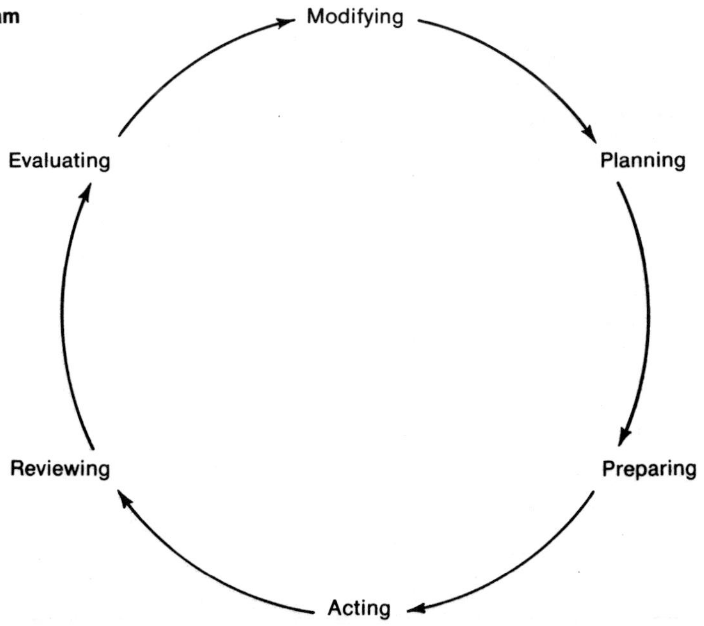

Fig.2.2 Membership of Work Groups

Complete the following:

"I am a member of the following work groups: (Write out under the headings the names of the groups using terms that are used in your agency. N.B. Some groups may be written under more than one heading. Decide which is the more appropriate.)

My primary work group, agency or team is . . . .

Case Conferences and Reviews

. . . .

Divisional or Area Management Meetings

. . . .

Inter-Agency and Interdisplinary Groups (specify)

. . . .

Management Committees (specify)
(including committees involving elected representatives)

. . . .

. . . .

Policy Development Groups (specify)
Trade Union Groups

. . . .

Working Parties (specify)

. . . .

Others (not included in the above headings)

. . . .

. . . .

. . . .

Professional Interest Groups

. . . .

Special-Interest Groups (specify)

. . . .

Staff Development and Supervision Groups

. . . .

Staff Group Meetings (e.g. team meetings, ward rounds)

. . . .

. . . .

. . . .

User or Consumer Groups (e.g. Tenants Association Residents Committee).

. . . .

b) The Need to Work on Different Group Functions

To be effective all groups have to work simultaneously with two kinds of tasks. The one kind are the instrumental tasks. They involve the means by which the group's explicit goals get accomplished. The other are the expressive tasks i.e. the activities that the goup engages in to express its concern and interest in those people directly or indirectly involved. This may entail encouraging individuals to work together or simply ensuring that opportunities exist for all group members to feel they are making a reasonable contribution that is valued. Thus how a group generates energy, enthusiasm and commitment to work tasks may depend on their feelings about the job in hand and about one another. In most work groups it is important to develop a climate of mutual consent and respect, which results in more effective work performance. (See d) below).

Fig. 2.3 (sometimes described as "the poached egg" model) suggests the different types of work in which members must engage to be an

effective group in both instrumental and expressive terms.[3] Circle (a) reflects the time and effort needed to carry out the instrumental goals of the group e.g. to discuss an item on the agenda and to reach a satisfactory conclusion. Circle (b) indicates the need for individuals to receive support from the rest of the group so that they can make an effective contribution; e.g. "Why do you seem so tired today?" The work here is described as individual maintenance activity. Circle (c) reflects the need of the group to pay attention to the way it works together and to its relationships as a group; e.g. "Why do we always seem to be fighting one another?" This is referred to as group maintenance activity.

All three kinds of work need to be undertaken to some degree. Many of the techniques described in Part II of this book demonstrate how instrumental and expressive activities can be carried out.

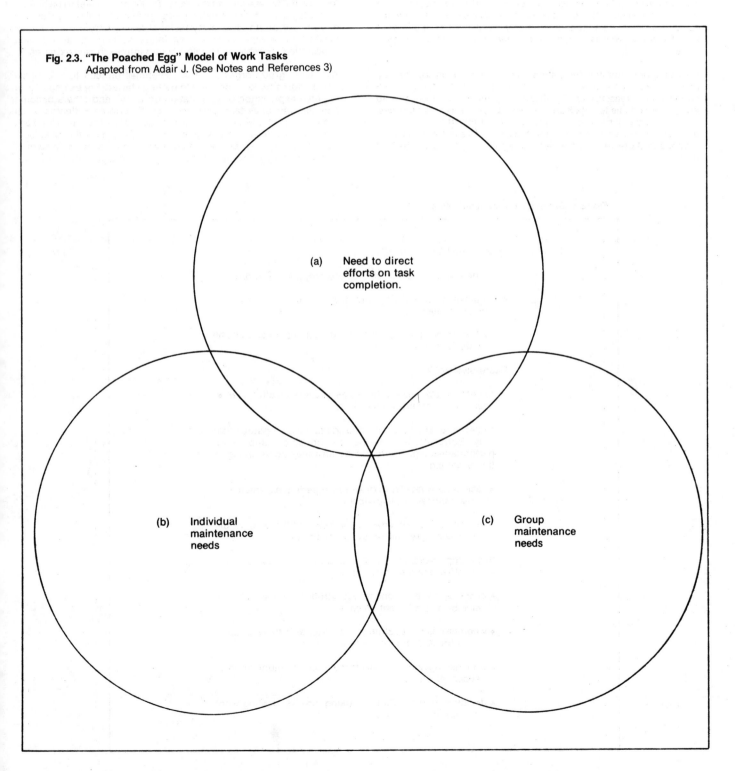

Fig. 2.3. "The Poached Egg" Model of Work Tasks
Adapted from Adair J. (See Notes and References 3)

(a) Need to direct efforts on task completion.

(b) Individual maintenance needs

(c) Group maintenance needs

c) Working on "beginnings", "middles" and "endings"

(i) Beginnings

"Beginning" work refers to the following situations:

— at the start of the life of a group (joining);

— at the beginning of a new session or meeting (rejoining);

— when starting a new agenda item (changing pace or style).

Fig. 2.4. gives goals and examples of activities which might be undertaken under any of these circumstances.

Though some techniques emphasise instrumental over expressive activities and vice-versa, in practice the two functions have usually to be carried out simultaneously. For example at the beginning of a meeting statements of expectations might include ideas about the outcomes which are sought (instrumental) and in terms of personal satisfaction or what is sought from other group members (expressive).

Providing opportunities for getting rid of emotional luggage can be important for some groups, not only to meet needs for personal support and reassurance (individual maintenance) but also to enable individuals to establish their own boundaries and priorities. In other words "What I need to put to one side for the next hour in order to make an effective contribution to this meeting is . . . ." "What might prevent me from making a full contribution is the fact that . . .".

Developing clear boundaries: similarly the establishment of a clear timetable and working arrangements will have value in terms of providing support and clarity, again assisting the development of boundaries. Questions to answer here include: "What will I be required to do?" "How much will I have to disclose or be exposed to others?" "How much should I already know?"

The development of boundaries helps to set the tone and prepares for later work. If boundaries are unclear and confusing at the start as a result of mixed or ambiguous messages having been sent, problems are likely to multiply at later stages. Joining experiences can also be recorded and used for later evaluation purposes in terms of "This is what I thought and felt at that time, these were my goals and expectations . . . This is what I think and feel now . . ."

Beginnings don't just happen. It is always important to remember, either as a leader or group member, that to begin a session, new agenda item etc, requires a conscious effort. Someone needs to be responsible for starting off the work. Participants need to be helped to identify goals, focus, muster energy and emotional resources. It is often important to clear away residual feelings from the previous meeting or session as these can influence current feelings and expectations. People need help to enter into each new experience.

As a work group organiser it is sometimes difficult to know how much effort should be devoted to getting started. For example, give too little explanation or information on a task and others become confused and uncertain. Give too much, boredom and deafness can easily set in, which can lead to resistance. Spend too much time on emotional expression and you may have too little for the task itself. But to leave feelings unacknowledged can lead to inefficient use of time and energy, because people do not "engage" (See Fig. 2.4.)

Fig. 2.4. Goals for "Beginning" Work

Instrumental Goals

— to identify goals and tasks for the group to work on

—· to develop a clear structure and plan of work including timetable, method etc.

— to identify individual goals and expectations, what each can contribute or not to the task

Expressive Goals

— to get to know one another as people, irrespective of what each can contribute to the task

— to get rid of any "emotional luggage" and pressures that may both affect working relationships and work performance e.g. any fears and anxieites about being in the group e.g.

  • residual feelings from previous experiences which might hinder participation

  • any doubts or personal assessments of the amount of energy people might have at that time

— to develop a specific culture and ways of working together, which affect the total process e.g.

  • declaring expectations about introducing new members at different times

  • whether it is felt desirable to remain as a total group or to break down into sub-groups

  • establishing norms about attendance, communication of absences etc

  • deciding on rules about smoking, breaks, dealing with disruptions

(ii) Middles — Assessing and Working on Problems

The middle phase can refer to (a) the time spent in working on the main problem(s) facing the group, (b) that part of a session or meeting, when the major work items are addressed, or (c) the concentration of energy on a single item or problem after it has been introduced. Again there are a vast number of management techniques designed to help work group members explore, assess, find solutions or responses to presenting problems and issues and to take effective decisions. But it is the processes by which group members engage and work toegther on tasks that provide the acid tests of participatory practice. In this book we have tried to put together management and educational problem-solving techniques in such ways that they encourage participation throughout the process and give an appropriate emphasis to both instrumental and expressive group functions.

The criteria used in the selection of techniques (see Part II) include the need to:

— unscramble problems together

— assist decision taking

— assist individual and group learning and development as a continuous process which is fully integrated into daily practice.

Assessing and resolving problems, taking decisions, planning further action are the instrumental processes that occupy work groups during these "middle" phases. Expressive activities are reflected in the members' interaction and involvement, mutual help and supportiveness, ability to face up to and confront differences openly, obtain acceptance and commitment to group decisions. It is important, however, to remember that many so-called problems beg perfect solution. In many cases it is a matter of working out what is better or worse in the circumstances and the "best fit" to meet the specific goals being pursued at the time. It is also important to build in means by which the process can be reviewed and evaluated so that "learning from experience" can take place. This is probably the best way of integrating learning and practice (see, for example, the exercise under Part II E, Reviewing Progress and Process).

(iii) Moving On

One problem facing many meetings is that of "moving on". Groups often become immersed in a particular problem and are reluctant to leave it either because it hasn't been solved in the time available or because consciously or otherwise members prefer to keep working at it. This reduces the priority of other items. The key to solving this kind of processual problem is to stick with the agreed timetable, not rigidly, but modifying it only with the full agreement of the group. In effect this might involve a simple vote "to work at this for another 15 minutes or to move on now". Sometimes of course the guillotine simply has to drop. It is salutory to remind ourselves that few human service decisions "wrap themselves up nicely" and incompleteness is something that has to be accepted sometimes.

(iv) Endings

By "endings" we can mean (a) bringing the working life of [...] an end; (b) finishing a meeting or session to be resumed on a [...] occasion, or (c) bringing a sense of closure as a boundary cond[...] to a particular topic or item so that work can begin on the next one.

Instrumental: the working during "end" phases is similar to that needed at the beginning. On the instrumental side, decisions have to be taken, actions planned, additional work tasks allocated. Loose ends have to be tied; people will need to be clear about any agreements or decisions which have been reached. It is always useful to check and reaffirm what has been decided. The questions to ask are:

— "What has been agreed, (proposed, recommended, decided) for this aspect of the work?"

— "Who has agreed to do what in terms of follow up or implementation?"

— "Have we got an accurate record of our decisions?"

— "How do we report back any progress or come back to this matter on a future occasion?"

Expressive: the expressive work focusses on how individuals and the group feel about what has gone on before, how they feel about any decision, have they something to get off their chests before they leave and move on to the next item. Which is likely to affect subsequent performances or future relationships? With groups that are finishing for good, the task is to work out how to say goodbye appropriately so that people actually experience the closure and are thus able to manage any residual feelings of separation and loss effectively. This leave taking is also important if individuals can expect to meet others again in a different work group situation as any residual feelings e.g. of anger may be carried over. Again the exercises and techniques described under "Endings" (Part II G) are all selected to achieve both instrumental and expressive purposes during the end phases.

d) Tasks and Skills in Working with Groups

In a hierachical work group most of the responsibility for planning and managing, that is in "making the group tick" rests with the formal leader. But even in this type of group the leader has still to work out ways and means of obtaining contributions and commitment from group members — other than through coercion and the threat of sanctions. Otherwise the leader is effectively left to do all of the work inside and outside the group. In contrast an assumption of a more participatory work style is that the felt as well as the actual responsibility for effective group performance rests with the group as a whole. A consequence of this approach is that what can be described as "chairperson skills" are often required by every member at one time or another. By chairperson skills we do not only refer to the more formal tasks of preparing agendas and taking decisions but to the work needed to manage the group process. (See Fig 2.5)

Fig. 2.5. Group Work Tasks

structuring —	providing structure and boundaries within which the group can work	reflecting —	drawing attention to or eliciting emotions and feelings that are affecting work relationships
focussing —	ensuring that the group maintains its focus on the task	creating —	encouraging creativity and originality
motivating —	encouraging and motivating one another to participate or contribute;	clarifying —	making explicit and overt what might remain unspoken, uncovering what is unhealthily implicit and covert e.g. hidden agendas
mediating —	mediating in or resolving conflict situations	directing —	identifying and assessing progress towards group goals
caretaking —	supporting and enabling people who are experiencing difficulty or stress		

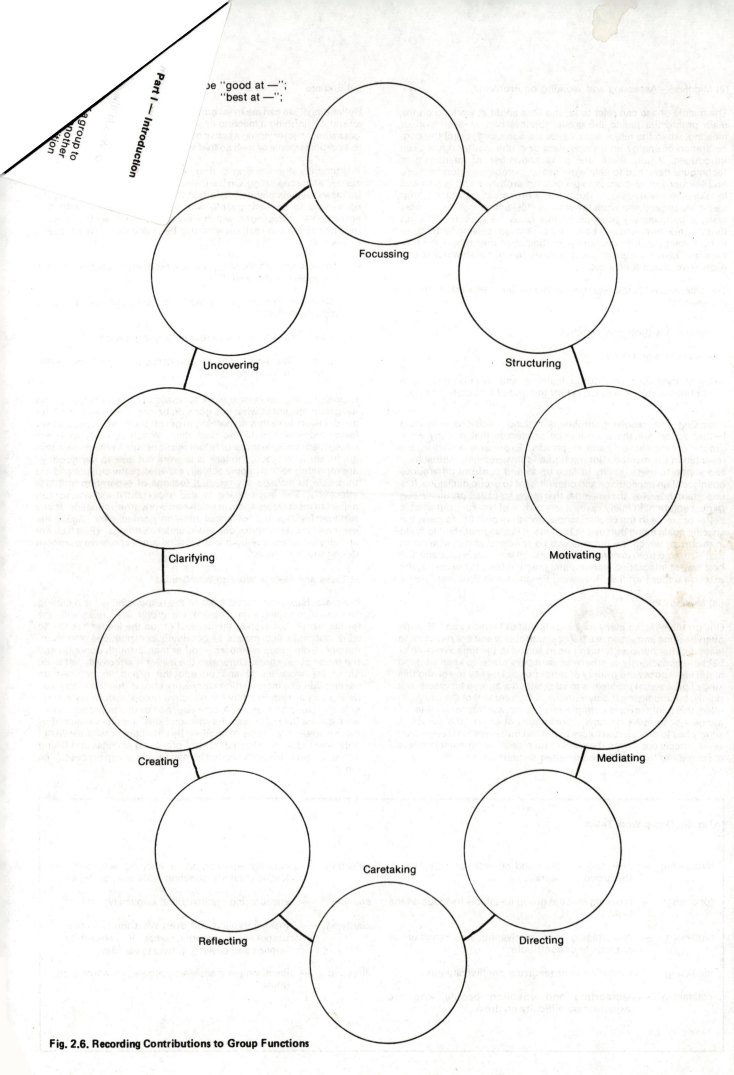

Focussing

Structuring

Uncovering

Clarifying

Motivating

Creating

Mediating

Reflecting

Caretaking

Directing

Fig. 2.6. Recording Contributions to Group Functions

The question "who does or should undertake" any of these tasks is always something for each group to work out for itself. In hierarchical groups it will be the formal leader or chairperson with perhaps only occasional contributions from other group members. However, the more "participatory" the group the more likely are tasks to be distributed amongst group members depending on who appears to be the most able and relevant person(s). Figure 2.6 provides a method of recording observations of which group members appear to take on what tasks. The questions "who appears to be good/best at . . ." can be used to focus observations. If used as an exercise with a particular work group we would expect the results to be discussed with group members and used to make explicit the different contributions that individuals do or might make to any of these tasks.

(i) Interpersonal Skills

The skills needed for effective work group practice are similar to those for any group work. Technical and interpersonal skills are required for completing various activities of planning, preparing, beginning, completing, reviewing and evaluating. Interpersonal skills are needed to enable group members to communicate with one another and to ensure that the tasks associated with the different group functions (instrumental and expressive) are carried out to everyone's satisfaction.

(ii) Receiving Skills

These include:

— listening carefully to what each other has to say

— trying to understand the feelings behind what is being said

— checking out statements to understand correctly and accurately that what is heard is what was said

— focussing and clarifying so that others are helped to communicate more effectively

— interpreting, checking out and making appropriate responses to non-verbal messages.

(iii) Feedback Skills

Another set of skills involves the ability to give appropriate feedback to people on what they are saying and on how they are performing in the group. Here it is important:

- to be constructively critical, commenting on what the other might do to change something as opposed to being purely destructive, with the intention of putting the person down (e.g. "What I think you might do to make your idea work is . . ." not "What a stupid idea . . .")

- to concentrate any personal feedback on behaviour rather than on whole personality and therefore avoid making moralistic sounding statements or personal judgements of others (e.g. "You haven't said anything so far . . ." not "Why are you such a lazy person . . .")

- to be responsible for what you yourself feel and think and do not project your feelings on to others (e.g. "I feel very angry about . . ." not "Everything about this group is so boring and dead"). Make your verbal and non-verbal messages consistent with one another (e.g. by saying something to one person and looking at her/him not at someone else!)[4]

e) Reviewing and Evaluating Work Groups

As a final exercise (Fig. 2.7) we provide a checklist of questions to enable the reader to review and evaluate any of the work groups to which she/he may belong. This can be used to help assess whether to introduce any of the contents of this guide and to indicate which techniques are likely to be useful and for what purposes.

Fig. 2.7. Checklist With Which To Review Your Different Work Groups

(i) Name of Group

Name of Group?

What are its purposes?

What are its specific goals?

What is the group composition?

What resources does it need and possess?

What are the roles or tasks of individual group members, e.g. who is responsible for structuring and planning the use of time?

What working methods or techniques are used?

(ii) Review of Processes

How would you assess its processess?

i.e. — How are tasks started, developed and completed?

— Who appear to get involved; who appear uninvolved?

— Who appear to act as important influences on the process and in what ways? What skills do they use?

— How are decisions usually taken? Do decisions get implemented?

— Are decisions and subsequent actions reviewed?

(iii) Review of Effectiveness

Is the group generally effective or not? Remember that to be effective a work group will need to assess:

— How well goals are accomplished (instrumental activities)

— How well the group maintains itself throughout its various tasks in terms of energy, drive, motivation, commitment, interest and mutual supportiveness (expressive activities)

Notes and References

1. For alternative definitions of teams and team-models see Payne C. and Scott T. **Developing Supervision of Teams In Field and Residential Social Work.** Part 1. National Institute for Social Work Papers No.12 London, NISW 1982.

2. See Miller C. and Scott T. **Strategies and Tactics. Planning and Decision Making in Social Services Teams.** National Institute For Social Work Papers No. 18 London, NISW 1985.

3. Adapted from Adair J. "Training leaders". Ch. 1. in Babington Smith and B.A. Farrell (Eds.) **Training in Small Groups. A Study of Five Methods.** Oxford, Pergamon Press 1979. p.9.

4. There are many books and articles that identify and describe how to develop interpersonal skills and those of receiving and giving feedback. See, for example, Egan G. **The Skilled Helper.** Monterey, California, Brooks/Cole 1982. Also Luft J. and Ingham H. "Effective Feedback" in **Basic Reader In Human Relations Training.. Part 1 Readings in Sensitivity Training.** New York, The Episcopal Church (undated). This last article gives some rules about personal disclosure and giving feedback based on a conceptual framework popularly known as the Johari Window.

CHAPTER 3

CHOOSING AND USING METHODS AND TECHNIQUES

a) Effective Management is Responsive Management.

In an educational or training setting it is relatively easy to choose a variety of working arrangements and processes to encourage active involvement of all participants in the task in hand. When planning for courses or events it is recognised that detailed consideration should be given to both content and process. This book has been prepared to help managers and others in their daily work to take advantage of these ideas to modify the way planning, negotiating, communicating and other interactive tasks are handled.

Unlike the trainer, the manager has often very little time to prepare and often has to react immediately in response to situations as they arise. This requires an effective manager to develop a repertoire of responses that can be brought into use as they appear to be needed.

(i) Taking risks

This means taking risks. For example, suggesting that the team or group should stop what it's doing and try to work "in this way ..." or to use "that approach ..." will require the initiator to stop the flow of discussion or debate and guide it along another path or via another process. It requires confidence to stop operating in the "way we've always done it" and propose an alternative approach or approaches. It also requires commitment to stick with new ways of working when people start to grumble or appear resistant to change.

(ii) Managing resistances to change

In choosing new approaches this resistance to change is often the greatest obstacle to overcome. The reasons are normally illogical and are relatively immune to rational argument. The experience of such changes suggest a "suck it and see" approach often succeeds in shifting at least some people's positions, but the main ingredients are commitment, confidence and stickability for the person or persons leading the change.

(iii) Involving the group in choosing and using

It is often necessary to develop co-operative or collaborative approaches to the introduction of new working practices. This suggests the team itself may need to be involved in the process of choosing and using different working processes. The idea of ownership is crucial here. Approaches that are understood and accepted by group members are much more likely to be used well than those suggested or imposed by individuals.

(iv) Think carefully before choosing

When the choice of working practices opens up there is a temptation to introduce so many that the meeting begins to look like a Christmas tree. Choosing one approach that works is likely to be much more effective than a variety that confuse. Introducing new ideas at appropriate moments is likely to encourage a greater chance of acceptance; expecting people in a team already under pressure for a decision to stop and change their working practices is probably futile.

The main criteria for choice should be based on the likelihood of the method or approach increasing the effectiveness and efficiency of analysis or decision making. Subsidiary criteria may also relate to energy levels or creativity or the expressive elements of work rather than the instrumental activities. By reading the briefing papers for each method or working arrangement it is possible to assess which type of criteria they are likely to meet in different settings at different times. It is possible that when you have used some approaches in the way we suggest, you will want to include them for entirely different reasons with other goals in mind. As all these approaches have been developed by people building on and modifying each other's ideas and experiences, your adaptions will be a logical extension of this work.

b) How to use the rest of the book

Part II of this book contains over 30 techniques and exercises that have been found useful as aids to obtaining participation in different kinds of group situations. Part III (Set Menus) provides examples of how combinations of techniques can be used for different purposes. All are taken from "real life" applications by the authors themselves.

Many of the techniques described will be recognisable as common training techniques. What we have tried to do is to adapt them for use in managing work groups as well as for training events. These are only a selection of techniques that can be used; chosen because the authors, the majority of whom occupy management positions in social services agencies, have found them to be useful and effective in their own practice. The contents are arranged so that they correspond to the main stages of a group's work. For example techniques to assist "getting started" are placed at the beginning followed by techniques for "middle-stage work", then "endings". The last two sections in Part II discuss some specific techniques (eg the use of visual aids) that can be used at any stage.

However this way of arranging the contents does not mean that there is any prescribed order for their use. For example, reviewing techniques can be used at the beginning or end of a group session or part way through in order to "move on". Neither is it expected that the user will want to apply every single technique. It is better to stick to a small number of well tried techniques with which the manager and group feels comfortable and which works for them than to use techniques for the sake of it. Some of the techniques included here apply to specific situations and for particular purposes; others may have a more general application.

(i) Guidelines

The rules of thumb are:

- Select or "dip in" to find what you need.

- Do not be frightened to modify or adapt any selected technique.

- Experiment from time to time with new techniques, when the need arises, but do not introduce them without a purpose.

Always remember that techniques by themselves will not increase participation, make for more effective decision-making etc. They are only means to those ends.

(ii) Format

Each technique is described in a set formula to assist in making the right choice. There is a short description of the technique followed by a statement of goals or objectives. The procedures to be followed in order to use the techniques are described next. Then a set of practical tips ("Do's and Don'ts") and finally a few guidelines on the kind of situations where the technique might be used with some examples from actual practice.

It will be seen that certain techniques are better used to get things going, while others particularly help with problem solving, or actually working on the tasks. Many of them are interchangeable. Hopefully the formula will encourage users to identify their objectives, which will then make choice easier. The formula also lists materials required, which indicate the amount of preparation and planning that might be required; lack of this is often the downfall of many a good intention.

(iii) Where to start

It must not be forgotten that the most commonly used method in groups is "free ranging" discussion. We would not wish to discourage debate and discussion on certain issues but suggest that by using techniques like the Nominal Group Technique (see Part II C) discussion methods can achieve a greater sense of purpose and discipline.

The message of this manual is take a risk and try some new methods of work. Start with those groups with which you feel familiar and comfortable and who would be prepared to allow you to try something new. Try where possible to select techniques that you feel confident in using, perhaps starting with something simple like brainstorming your next staff meeting agenda, using a fishbowl as an aid to interviewing candidates for a post or the nominal group technique. Try where possible to use the simpler techniques with larger groups, and gradually build up your repertoire, rather than thinking you have to jump in at the deep end and worry that you'll sink. Feel free to adapt the methods to meet your own working situations, and good luck.

PART II
METHODS AND TECHNIQUES
(Individual Recipes)

CONTENTS

A. SETTING THE AGENDA   27

    1. Pre-set agendas

    2. Setting an agenda "on the spot"

    3. Setting an agenda with a new group

B. EFFECTING INTRODUCTIONS   31

    4. The name game

    5. Introduce your partner

    6. Using a personal disclosure checklist

C. MAKING MORE EFFECTIVE USE OF GROUP RESOURCES   35

    7. Forming sub-groups

    8. Buzz groups

    9. Group chairing

    10. Fishbowls

D. ASSESSING AND WORKING ON PROBLEMS   41

    11. Nominal group techniques

    12. Brainstorming

    13. Role play

    14. Sculpting

    15. Flow charting

E. REVIEWING PROGRESS AND PROCESS   53

    16. Reviewing and appraisal techniques

    17. Techniques for giving and receiving feedback to a group

F. TAKING DECISIONS BY VOTING   59

    18. How to use voting procedures

G. ENDINGS   61

    19. Drawing shields

    20. The cocktail party

    21. Guided phantasy

    22. Action planning

    23. Forming networks

H. USING AUDIO/VISUAL AIDS   69

    24. Art gallery

    25. Presenting and displaying information

    26. Using tapes and slides (audio tapes, video tapes, tape slide
        sets, films)

I. FOCUSSING AND STRUCTURING TECHNIQUES   79

    27. Trigger sentences

    28. Briefing notes and handouts

    29. Planning frameworks

    30. Listing and clustering

    31. Using "pattern" recording techniques

SECTION A   SETTING THE AGENDA

The agenda or programme provides a structure to indicate the goals, tasks and sometimes the methods to be used at meetings or sessions of the work group. How an agenda is set and by whom are important indications of the levels of participation and control which a group is able to achieve.

It is important for work group members to be as involved in the practice of setting the agenda as it is in theory. Genuine participation will not be achieved if the agenda is always left to the chairperson or dominant individuals, who are able then to manipulate the content of the meeting for their own ends. Working relationships can deteriorate when a group feels it is exploited or that the real issues are not being addressed. It introduces "hidden agendas" or sets out to reject proposals, which if introduced differently, might have been accepted.

Everyone has a responsibility for contributing to the agenda. The work group leader or co-ordinator has an additional responsibility for enabling contributions to be made.

In this section 3 procedures for setting an agenda are described according to the different circumstances under which meetings take place.

Contents

1. Pre-set Agendas   28

2. Setting an Agenda "on the spot"   29

3. Setting an Agenda with a new group   29

Part II — Methods and Techniques

1. PRE-SET AGENDAS

Description

Agenda setting refers to the process of deciding the

- contents
- sequence
- duration

of items for consideration by a meeting. It is an important process because a poorly formed agenda will obscure the purpose of a meeting, or use time inefficiently because the most relevant items are given insufficient consideration.

Objectives

1. To determine the items to be discussed.

2. To determine the amount of time, actual or relative, to be given to each item.

3. To allow background information to be prepared or considered prior to the meeting.

4. To ensure that individual items are given the appropriate treatment during a meeting in terms of time spent etc.

Procedures

1. Members of the group are asked to submit items for the agenda by a given date before the meeting, either verbally, in writing or on sheet posted in a convenient place.

2. A person submitting an agenda item should be encouraged to provide accompanying background/briefing notes.

3. Procedures for putting items into sequence may include:

   a) random allocation of items
   b) the order in which items are received
   c) in order of importance, as perceived by the convenor/chairperson. Time can be allocated for each item if this helps to structure the meeting.

4. A copy of the agenda, together with any briefing material should be sent to all members of the group before the meeting with the expectation that they will read and prepare for it.

5. At the meeting the chair person/convenor proceeds to consider the items in the agreed agenda order.

Do's and Don'ts

- It is always useful to review an agenda at the beginning of the meeting so that group members are clear about what is to be discussed, the order of priority of items and the amount of time to be allocated to each one. Some items may be renegotiated on the basis of this discussion. An Any Other Business (AOB) slot is useful but must not become the focus for all late items. Only accept issues that must be dealt with now.

- It is useful to follow a regular planning cycle. A monthly cycle might thus:

  (a) circulate minutes/notes during week following the last meeting
  (b) agree a deadline for agenda items, say 7 days before the next meeting
  (c) circulate the agenda and any briefing notes, say 3-4 days before the meeting.

Briefing Notes

Issue guidelines for notes, to include:

- a description of the problem/issue, including where possible a historical perspective, present policy, what goes for custom and practice, examples based on precedent.

- The facts operating in the present situation or case.

- Opinions and judgements based on the facts.

- Possible options available for consideration with their implications.

- Recommendations as to the preferred option.

Presenting an Agenda

Include:

- Date and place of meeting

- Chairperson's name

- Apologies for absence

- Minutes

- Matters arising

- Correspondence

- Agenda items

- Date and place of next meeting

- Any other business, as a rule this should be for minor or urgent items only.

Writing up Minutes/Notes

Include:

- Name of group. Date and place of meeting. Chairperson.

- Members present: full name and position. Others present e.g. guest speaker.

- Apologies for absence.

- All items should have a clear heading and number.

- It is usual to write in third person, past tense.

- Minutes should be as brief as possible, commensurate with covering salient points. Papers circulated with agenda eliminate need for introductory material.

- Try to summarise what is said e.g. "Mr. K. raised the question of ......" rather than "Mr. K. said ......" and almost verbatim report.

- Avoid minuting explanations, side issues, anecdotes, departures from the subject, gathering of thoughts etc.

- Minutes should finish with conclusions or recommendations (and to whom they are addressed) or decisions. It might be useful to have an action column on one side of the paper. This allows rapid reference and monitoring at next meeting.

When to Use

- Any regular staff meeting to discuss progress and current issues.

- Any meeting to discuss a specific problem/set of proposals where focus and content can be anticipated in advance.

2. SETTING AN AGENDA "ON THE SPOT"

When there is no pre-set agenda the following procedures can be used:

1. Members are asked to suggest items for consideration. These should be displayed on the wall, large sheet of paper or overhead projector etc.

2. Members are then asked to state which items should be given most priority.

3. Members should establish time boundaries: a) an overall time limit for the meeting, and b) time limits for each agenda item. If there are too many items, rather than prolong the meeting beyond the agreed time, it is better to consider either reducing the time allocated to each item, or arranging a further meeting.

4. Notes should be kept of any decisions that are made and of who is responsible for any action.

When To Use

eg. An ad hoc meeting called to discuss a sudden occurrence or set of issues, which cannot wait until the next scheduled meeting.

Example: Daily Team Meeting Agenda

4. Discussion of firelighting incident (JS. CB)
1. Weekend arrangements (AC)
2. Staff cover for group at camp (AC)
3. Next week's staff training session (DB)

↑

order of discussion

---

3. SETTING AN AGENDA WITH A NEW GROUP

With a group meeting for the first time some additional procedures are important:

1. Members should be introduced to one another and basic information exchanged
i.e. names, organisations represented, interests in taking part in the meeting.

2. The group should clarify the purpose of the meeting and any terms of reference which may be laid down.

3. Ways of working and procedures have to be agreed and established.

Some time spent on each of these 3 areas will be well spent and make subsequent discussion easier.

When to use

— Meetings of people to explore the possibility of setting up a more permanent group e.g. a common interest group, support network.

— A meeting of people from different sections/agencies called to examine some new proposals/common problems, e.g. an inter-agency meeting to examine intermediate treatment policies and provisions; child-abuse procedures; collaboration between district health and personal social services over places in Part III accommodation etc.

Note

See also Section H (Using Audio/Visual Aids) for techniques to assist presentation and public displays of agendas.

SECTION B   INTRODUCTIONS

This section is included to help new groups form and get started in their work together. The techniques described are commonly known in training manuals as "ice-breakers", of which there are many more examples.

Their purposes are to help the members of a new work group get to know one another and to develop trust so that they can release energy to work on the tasks. Groups that have a limited amount of time may need to effect the introductions reasonably quickly. But the time is well spent in making the group more efficient if members are able:

— to know who the other members are; where they come from; what their interests are, etc.

— to state their personal goals and expectations of the group.

— to say something about themselves which will make working together easier.

The techniques described in Section E can als o be used to achieve this last objective.

Contents

4. The Name Game   32

5. Introduce your Partner   33

6. Using a Personal Disclosure Checklist   34

4. THE NAME GAME
(Never assume that people know who the others are)

Description

An exercise to introduce group members to one another in order to assist identification and remembering names.

Objectives

1. To help people remember who's who in the group.

2. To allow people to unwind.

3. To inject a note of humour into the proceedings at an early stage.

Procedures

1. Seat the group in a circle/oval.

2. Choose a person from anywhere in the room to introduce him/herself e.g. Q. "Say who you are"; A "I am Mary Jones".

3. Ask Mary Jones to "pass it on" to the left/right.

4. That person introduces her/himself etc and is also asked to say who the first person is e.g. "I am Bill Smith and this is Mary Jones".

5. The third person is asked to remember the first two people's names in addition to giving her/his own i.e. "I am Betty Bruce, this is Bill Smith and that is Mary Jones".

6. Every person is subsequently asked to identify and repeat the names of everyone who has been introduced previously in addition to giving his/her own name until the circle has been completed.

Additional Procedures

● Accept "cheating", for example, when people start to write down names or tick off against a membership list; anything to assist recognition is to be encouraged.

● The chain can be broken by stopping at the half way point and re-starting at the other end; thus building a new chain to the point where it was previously stopped. This is done without previous warning and usually causes a great deal of laughter; relief for some, sudden panic for others.

● It is useful if the group leader/facilitator takes part in the exercise. It helps to establish his/her identification with the group.

Do's and Don'ts

● There may be initial resistance, usually quickly dispelled once the "game" is under way.

● Some people may be shy of speaking in a large group — this usually helps them to overcome their inhibitions.

● It may be thought to be time wasting — 20-30 minutes may be needed for a large group. Keep introductions brief i.e. no more than name and position.

When to Use

Any training event/meeting where it cannot be assumed that participants know one another by name; where people are expected to work together for some considerable time and a sense of familiarity needs to be promoted.
e.g. At the start of — a short course (on any topic)
                     — a newly convened working party/committee
                     — an in-agency day conference/study day

The exercise is more suitable for a largish group eg 30. With large numbers it is better to introduce people to one another in sub-groups or not at all. It is less suitable when a limited amount of time is available.

It has however, been used with groups from the same agency and even the same residential establishment with a particularly large staff group!

The Name Game

5. INTRODUCE YOUR PARTNER
(Now I know something about you and ...)

Description

This exercise enables each individual to get to know one or two other people in the group before being introduced to the wider group. As the title suggests the basic idea is for one person to be introduced by another to the group after some brief discussion in pairs or trios.

Objectives

1. To faciltate introductions in the larger arena by holding discussions in smaller groups first.

2. To allow individuals to become more fully acquainted with one or two members of a group, which otherwise might remain impersonal.

3. To activate skills in listening, remembering and communicating, which might be inhibited in a larger group atmsophere.

Procedures

1. At the beginning of the meeting participants are asked to introduce themselves to either one or two other people in the group. e.g. "Introduce yourself to your neighbour". "Introduce yourself to the people on either side of you."

2. People may also be briefed to: say where they come from; what they do; their reasons for being there; their personal goals and expectations.

3. At the end of a given time (usually not more than 5 minutes) the group reconvenes.

4. Each person is then asked to introduce her/his partner or (in the case of a threesome) one of the other two people with whom the discussion was held.
e.g. "May I introduce . . . . . . She works as . . . . . .at . . . . . . She is here because . . . . . . What she wants from this group/meeting is . . . . . .

5. NB. Some statements may need to be verified by the person in question.

6. Some public recording of statements may be undertaken e.g. on flipcharts where it is important to have further discussion of personal goals and expectations.

Do's and Don'ts

— Keep the number of discussion points to maximum necessary: Usually name, position, personal goals and expectations, plus brief personal details if relevant.

— End the exchange by summarising any trends and important statements that have been made.

— Don't run over the time limit.

When to Use

This exercise can be used as an alternative to "The Name Game". It is equally effective with small groups. In a large group people might be asked to introduce their partners after entering a "fishbowl" (see C 10) before discussion takes place.

Introduce your partner.

6. USING A PERSONAL DISCLOSURE CHECKLIST
(This is what I want you to know about me . . .)

Description

The "personal disclosure cheaklist" provides a focussed way of enabling individuals to be introduced to the group. It encourages participants to think of statements about themselves i.e. who they are, why are they there, which might be of relevance to other members of the group in terms of future tasks and/or group maintenance activities. Examples of checklist items are given in the accompanying diagram. Checklists should be constructed to meet specific requirements. Where the checklist includes statements of personal goals it can also be used to review progress at later stages.

Objectives

1. To allow participants to reflect on what they need to disclose of themselves when being introduced in a new group.

2. To facilitate the exchange of personal goals and expectations of the group.

3. To provide a means by which group tasks and processes can be reviewed at a later stage.

Procedures

1. Group members are asked to think about and write down their responses to a given set of questions (The ground rules given in Section D for Nominal Group Techniques should be applied).

2. The checklist items can be presented on a flip chart/board or as a prepared questionnaire. (See Section H)

3. On completion of the checklist individuals either exchange their answers in the wider group or discuss in pairs/small groups before a wider exchange. With a larger group a chaining approach is recommended (See Section C).

Do's and Don'ts

— Keep the checklist brief: no more than five items as a rule, fewer if possible.

— Use open ended questions rather than complete statements (See examples).

— Ask that answers are kept brief so that discussion takes place within the time limit.

— Ensure that each person has an equal opportunity for disclosure.

When to Use

— Personal disclosure checklists can be used on any training/workshop event, sometimes in addition to/instead of "The Name Game" (or similar introductory exercises).

— They are particularly useful in meetings or small groups where there is no pre-set agenda and where it is important to get people's expectations "out in the open" e.g. in a staff meeting; supervision session.

Examples of Personal Disclosure Checklists:

1. General

My name is . . . .

My job/role is . . . .

My employers are . . . .

My place of employment is . . . .

My personal interests are . . . .

. . . .

2. Goal Statements

What I want this group to achieve is . . . .

. . . .

My personal goals for this group are . . . .

. . . .

My expectations are that we will . . . .

. . . .

3. Group Items

The ways of working which I prefer are . . . .

. . . .

What I need by way of support from this group is . . . .

. . . .

What I think I can give to this group is . . . .

. . . .

SECTION C   MAKING MORE EFFECTIVE USE OF GROUP RESOURCES.

Group discussions are effective only when one person is able to speak in turn and others listen. But how often have we taken part in meetings which because they are badly focussed or conducted, disintegrate and several conversations go on simultaneously? Much frustration and anger is often generated when people for whatever reason are unable to have their say and feel that what they are saying is not being heard. Valuable contributions are often lost because discussion is dominated by one or two members, who may or may not stick to the point and others cannot get a word in edgeways.

The techniques described in this section are aimed at improving group effectiveness and achieving greater participation by providing structured opportunities for members to work for some of the time in sub-groups. This tactic has the effect of increasing the range and variety of contributions. It also encourages individuals who may be inhibited or prevented from contributing in the wider group to state their points of view.

Contents

7.   Forming Sub Groups   36

8.   Buzz Groups   36

9.   Group Chaining   37

10. Fishbowls   38

7. FORMING SUB-GOUPS
(Working in twos, threes and fours etc)

Description

A means of making more productive use of a group's resources by dividing into sub-groups (pairs, fours, etc) for specific purposes. Each sub-group may be given the same or different tasks. Agreements are needed with the sub-groups about time to be spent on tasks and methods for reporting back. The use of sub-groups is a useful way of getting an initial assessment of issues and a means of getting everyone involved in the task.

Objectives

1. To make effective use of a group's analytical and problem-solving resources by dividing tasks.

2. To create manageable work groups for specific tasks and purposes.

3. To clarify ideas or to take thinking a stage forward as a result of information presented in the larger group.

4. To prepare material for discussion in the wider group.

Procedures

1. Divide the group into smaller work groups, give each a brief and instructions for reporting back to the larger group.

2. Check that work groups are clear about their task and have appropriate ways of working.

3. Arrange for reporting back at the appropriate time.

4. Receive reports from sub-groups.

5. Discuss next stages.

Criteria for Group Formation

Several ways can be used to form the sub groups, eg:

— self-selection
— random allocation
— common interests
— ability to "get on" with one another
— ensuring that people with relevant knowledge and skills are appropriately placed.

Arrangements are needed about the criteria to be used in selection of groups. Criteria used should be explicit.

Do's and Don'ts

— Ensure that there is enough space for groups to work in and that they have adequate resources e.g. paper, pens and chairs etc.

— Ensure that a clear briefing is given for the material to be reported back; keep it succinct e.g. "Each group to record 3 major issues".

— Be prepared for rumblings and grumblings when group members are asked to change seats and move into a small group arrangement, where they are expected to do some work.

— Always check that the sub-groups are clear about their task. Be prepared to facilitate their working together. Some get bogged down or stuck in their own internal group process.

— Choose the size of the group carefully i.e. as to whether people should work in twos, threes or fours. The size will depend on the nature of the task and the circumstances.

— Composition is also important. Ensure that there is an appropriate "mix" in each group.

— Be cautious about always choosing group members. Often they can choose effective group combinations themselves.

When to Use

Any meeting or work group can sub-divide at any point in time to work on a common task. Each can have a different task, depending on what is required. Examples include:

— The chairperson of the staff meeting asks pairs/trios to produce a list of ideas about a particular proposal

— Participants in a training session are asked to break into sub-groups to discuss and give feedback on a given topic.

— At a meeting of residents/clients/tenants' association, small groups are asked to produce a list of items for the agenda, issues for discussion, viewpoints etc. for further consideration in the wider group

— A working party agrees to spend the next session working in sub-groups on a set task before reporting back to the total group at the following meeting

— Additionally sub-groups may be asked to work on the same task where a variety of views are needed.

8. BUZZ GROUPS
(Getting quickly to the topic . . .)

Description

A means by which people in a large group can give an initial response to a topic or questions by talking in small groups (hence the word "buzz"). Buzz groups can be used at the beginning of a meeting to obtain people's views and expectations of themselves and/or the group task or to break the monotony of a longer talk or discussion. Buzz groups are not intended to provide in-depth discussion, but a quick reaction to a given topic.

Objectives

1. To give group members an opportunity to give a sharp response to an issue or question by discussing it in a small group before discussion in the bigger group.

2. To get people participating who might otherwise not be involved.

3. To stimulate awareness of an issue and encourage participants to share ideas and reactions.

4. To produce reactions and results quickly.

Procedures

1. Participants are asked to join with others in small groups — maximum 5 persons to "buzz". They should remain in the same room.

2. A time limit is set.

3. Group leader or event organiser should clearly state the task, time limit and method of feedback.

4. Feedback should be limited to a number of key points — time must be allocated for feedback.

Do's and Don'ts

— Do not allow the buzz group to go on too long. This defeats the purpose. 5-10 minutes is the maximum.

— Watch for individuals who dominate discussion, even though time is limited.

— Negative ideas or feelings can easily be reinforced by group pressures. These may need to be exposed and handled in the feedback.

— Keep the buzz groups in one room to avoid splintering. The groups need to be seen as sub-groups of the total group throughout.

— Because time is limited, keep tasks simple. Address one issue at a time. If necessary have another round of "buzzing" if a second set of issues needs to be addressed.

When to Use

During any group session/meeting when a quick reaction is needed to a topic, or, for example, when a discussion has got "stuck".

Examples

— A staff meeting wants to get some ideas flowing about revising the rota system (or similar proposals).

— A supervision/support group spends the first 5 minutes of the session "buzzing" to produce a list of items for the agenda.

— Participants of a short course/training session break into buzz groups to evaluate the impact.

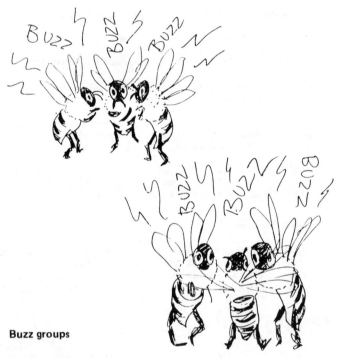

Buzz groups

9. GROUP CHAINING
"2 — 4 — 6 — 8"

Description

A variation of working in sub-groups. In successive stages individuals come together first as pairs, then as fours (2 pairs), and then as eights (2 fours) etc. This exercise is often used at the beginning of a training event as an "ice-breaker", but can be adapted to small group working and used to bring individuals into contact with the views of other group members in a structured way.

Objectives

1. To introduce individuals progressively to other group members.

2. To share an individual's own work, by stages, with the other group members.

3. To ensure all group members become involved in the session.

4. To enable individuals to build, develop and clarify ideas.

5. To allow individuals to see other perspectives on a subject.

6. To compare the different group processes at work in different sized groups.

Procedures

1. Individuals complete a piece of work for a set time period on their own
   e.g. a short questionnaire/personal disclosure checklist.

2. On completion each person finds a partner
   "Find someone you have never worked with before; introduce yourselves."
   "Find someone from the same or with a different professional background, introduce yourself and discuss your questionnaire response."

3. The pairs discuss their work, each giving the other time to disclose what she/he has done.

4. Ask pairs to form a four and repeat stages 2 and 3 with possibly some variations of task.

5. Fours then combine to form eights and continue their discussion.

Instead of forming an eight, representatives may be chosen from each of the fours to discuss their findings in an open/closed fishbowl (See C 10).

Do's and Don'ts

— The noise level may be excessive in a large group, which means that discussion is either superficial or non-productive. Find enough space for groups to work in comfortably.

— The constant forming and re-forming of groups can be frustrating for some and may prevent people from getting into the task. Provide opportunities in the final discussion for people to express any frustrations with the process.

— The technique should not be used for in-depth explanations of issues.

When to Use

This technique is more likely to be used as the start of a training event/workshop/conference so that people can gradually work their way into the larger groups and increase their range of contacts. Examples include:

Group Chaining

— at the beginning of a study day to bring together people with a common interest in a particular subject and method of intervention, e.g. on Intermediate Treatment, Child Abuse, Mental Health etc.

— at the beginning of an open evening for members of a Local Council of Voluntary Services or similar type of event.

— carrying out a preliminary study of a team's objectives by getting individuals to write out a list, then to share with a partner, small group and eventually the total group.

10. FISHBOWLS

Description

Arrangements for organising discussion with participants seated in concentric rings facing inwards are called fishbowls. People in the inner ring are expected to discuss a topic observed by those in the outer rings (or rings). Contributions from those in the outer ring are limited according to whether the fishbowl is "open" or "closed". The inner ring is formed by self-selection or pre-determined criteria.

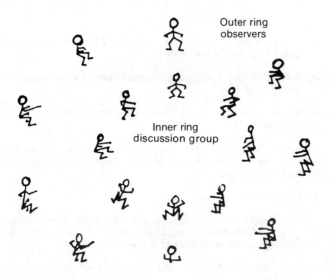

Outer ring observers

Inner ring discussion group

Objectives

1. To create a small group exchange within a larger group.

2. To structure the exchange of information as an alternative to a free-ranging discussion.

3. To give group members an opportunity of listening to what others are saying.

4. To allow time for reflection on issues before making their contribution.

5. To build on previous contributions by dividing a group into discussants and listeners and then reversing roles.

6. To provide opportunities for reflection and feedback on group process.

(i) Closed Fishbowl

This is used:

a) to disclose information from a small group to a larger group with no interaction allowed between groups during the process.

b) to enable people who may have something controversial or delicate to discuss, to consider the issues without interruption and engagement with others.

Procedures

1. The number of participants can be varied from having two or three in the inner ring (fishbowl) to eight to ten.

2. The number of people in the outer ring may be equal or larger than the inner ring, depending on the circumstances.

3. Ground rules must be established and adhered to i.e.

   a) a time limit set for each discussion.

   b) it is agreed whether to use an "open" or "closed" fishbowl arrangment (see below)

4. The exact number of chairs needed for participants are placed in the inner ring.

5. The centre fishbowl is then formed by asking for volunteers or directing people to sit in the fishbowl.

6. a) Group members take their seats sitting in a circle.

   b) Other members sit around the "outer circle".

   c) The two circles should have a clear space between them.

7. The topic/issue to be discussed is announced and the time limit given (10 minutes is often enough).

8. The observers remain silent during the proceedings but they may be asked to observe specific elements of the process or content for discussion later.

9. The fishbowl discussion takes place — no comments, interuptions or distractions are permitted from the outer group. The organiser calls time as agreed.

(ii) Open Fishbowl

This is used to enable members of the outer ring to make comments on the content and process of the fishbowl discussion and provides a step between closed discussion and full group interchange. A longer time is usually needed than for the closed fishbowl, e.g. 20 - 30 minutes.

Procedures

1. Additional chairs are added to the inner ring (usually no more than two) to enable interchange between the observers and inner circle.

2. A member of the outer ring who wishes to make a comment or raise a question is entitled to leave her/his chair and sit within the inner ring.If she/he does so, conversation should stop and the point be made quickly and concisely. No discussion with the outside is allowed and the observer must leave the ring after making his/her point.

3. The discussion continues as before. Members of the inner circle have discretion to take account of the contribution or ignore it as they choose.

Do's and Don'ts

— Distinguish clearly the type of fishbowl and the rules to be applied. Announce timings and make sure that the person responsible for managing the discussion is identified. Arrange for the "inner ring" to have a chairperson if appropriate (it is not usually necessary). Provide the observers with a clear brief.

— Make sure that those in the "outer ring" can hear the discussion. It is very frustrating when members of the "inner ring" talk in whispers or mumble. Ensure that the observers do not distract the people in the fishbowl by laughing, interruptions etc.

— Ensure that the task is clear; otherwise the discussion tends to wander. Allow time for de-briefing and review, particularly where sensitive and volatile issues are being discussed.

— Up to ten people can be asked to join the "inner ring"; more reduces the potential for participation. A smaller number, say five to eight, is preferable.

— Ensure that the methods used are appropriate to the topic and the required outcomes.

When to Use

— As a planning or reviewing tool e.g. a central group of working party members might discuss their findings in "open" or "closed" fishbowls in the presence of an audience of other colleagues.

— As a way of getting sub-groups to report back to the total group its conclusions or findings on a particular subject e.g. at a staff meeting.

— As a way of de-briefing training exercises which use small group work; small groups or representatives from the group meet in a fishbowl to discuss their work and conclusions.

— To structure certain types of role play (See D 13).

Fishbowls

SECTION D   ASSESSING AND WORKING ON PROBLEMS

This section contains no more than a sample of some of the more common methods and techniques from adult learning and management development sources, that can be used selectively by work groups to assess and find solutions to problems and issues.

They can be used in relation to one or more of the following:

— collecting views and information about a given subject

— making an assessment of the issues

— deciding what the priority issue(s) should be

— developing a range of possible solutions to problems /issues

— choosing the most appropriate solution

— reviewing and evaluating the decision(s) that have been taken

— rehearsing a particular course of action.

Contents

11.	Nominal Group Techninque	42
12.	Brainstorming	42
13.	Role Play	44
14.	Sculpting	49
15.	Flow Charting	50

11. NOMINAL GROUP TECHNIQUE

Description

The "Nominal Group Technique" (NGT) was developed by Delbecq and Van de Ven at the University of Wisconsin, Madison[1]. They defined a nominal group as "a method in which individuals work in the presence of others but do not verbally interact". The authors developed this method for participative planning and problem solving.

Research by the originators has suggested that the nominal method is superior to group interaction approaches, including brainstorming (see D 12), in producing a larger number of qualitatively superior ideas. Like brainstorming, the nominal method allows expression of minority opinions, unconventional and seemingly incompatible or conflicting ideas. The method also ensure maximum participation of group members, who operate as equals. It is thus particularly useful for obtaining participation in a mixed status group or one that tends to be dominated by powerful individuals or cliques.

Nominal work can often be done at the beginning or during a meeting/group session as an alternative to buzz groups and brainstorming. The value of the nominal group technique is that it gets people working and involved with the task in hand quickly, providing a basis for analysis and a focus for discussion. Writing down ideas promotes clarity of thought and reflective thinking as well as being an aid to creativity.

Ground Rules

Whether used as a simple technique to initiate group discussion or as the primary mode of working in planning, the principles and rules are the same viz:

— Individuals should work privately and silently for a given time. It is very important to ensure that there are no distractions while this work is going on.

— Ideas should preferably be written down, on cards or paper provided for the purpose so that everyone is working within the same boundaries and under identical conditions.

— Statements should be recorded verbally in round-robin fashion, preferably one per person at a time, until all are publicly recorded and displayed.

— No discussion is allowed until all statements are recorded thus. There will, however, be occasions when these rules are modified e.g. nominal work may be done verbally with each person speaking in turn. Here it is important to ensure that every person has an opportunity to speak unhindered before further group discussion.

Objectives

1. To start things off in a non-threatening manner by creating some space for people to think about issues.

2. To ensure that all individuals are allowed to contribute equally and without pressure or interference from other group members.

3. To collect some formal imput from all group members in a containable form

4. To help people think clearly about what they meant to say and to focus their thoughts.

5. To prepare individuals for a later discussion.

Procedures

1. Group members are asked to state and preferably write down their ideas on a subject with an agreed limit, say no more than 20 words or a set time. The task can be introduced by a "trigger" e.g. "One thing I want to find out about this subject is . . . . ."

2. Each person then reads out his/her responses, which can also be recorded on board, large sheets or overhead projector.

3. The combined statements can then be discussed and processed according to the purpose of the exercise.

Do's and Don'ts

— Consider in advance the best method for recording and how the feedback information is to be used. People will be frustrated if material is recorded and then neglected.

— Do not allow too much time for any one set of statements/ideas, otherwise recording and sorting becomes difficult. Maintain strict boundaries e.g. 2 minutes or one page of writing.

— Make sufficient time for recording (where undertaken) and for discussion afterwards.

When to Use

Nominal work can be used at any time in a meeting/session for a variety of tasks e.g.

— to identify the goals and expectations of participants at the start of a training exercise/supervision session/meeting using for example Personal Disclosure Checklist (See B6).

— to assist the assessment of a problem/issue during a staff meeting etc. by asking participants to write down and then state their views.

— to obtain a range of possible solutions/recommendations/ actions over a given problem by participants writing down their ideas prior to discussion (e.g. "Each person should make a list of three possible actions that we can take . . . .").

Notes and References

1. See Delbecq A. and Van de Ven H. "A group process model for problem identification and program planning" Ch.24 In N. Gilbert and H. Specht **Planning for Social Welfare. Issues, Models and Tasks.** New Jersey: Prentice Hall 1977 pp 333-348

12. BRAINSTORMING

One of the many lateral thinking techniques publicised by De Bono [1] but orginating in the 30's, brainstorming has come to be used extensively in problem-solving, educational and training contexts. The aim is for a group of people given a problem or focus to produce an array of possible solutions or statements in a short time by pouring out ideas that come to mind; irrespective of the apparent relevance or irrelevance of those ideas. The brainstorming rules encourage the production of novel, original and "way out" responses, which can be addressed more reflectively in subsequent analysis and discussion. The brainstorming principle rests on a free floating association of ideas that take issues beyond their conventional frame of reference. Though developed as a group method, it can be adapted by small groups of two or three people and in private work. It can be used to assess the possible causes of problems as well as to find solutions.

Objectives

1. To generate quickly a variety of ideas as perspectives for later analysis.

2. To liven up a group by providing a shared experience.

3. To list all the available options and ideas open to a group.

Procedures

1. One person acts as recorder

2. Present the problem or topic and go through the ground rules. These can be summarised in terms of Suspend Judgement, Free Wheel, Quantity, Cross-Fertilise.

a) Group members responses are recorded without comment or modification.

b) Other group members may add to a comment but not delete or alter a previous one.

c) All viewpoints are recorded including those that appear to be similar, contradictory or off the target.

d) The exercise continues until there are no more suggestions, no more space for recording or when a set time has elapsed (whatever has been agreed at the beginning).

Note: The process should be carried out quickly and non-reflectively. There is no discussion during the brainstorming on anyone's contribution. It is useful to carry out a short "warm up" e.g. on a "wild" topic before the brainstorm proper. It is important that the topic is clearly understood/defined and the use of a "trigger sentence" is often useful (see below).

Do's and Don'ts

— Brainstorming can generate too much material, which cannot be digested; this problem can be overcome by limiting the time/number of responses e.g. by saying "We stop after 5 minutes....... or after 20 minutes........ or after one sheet of paper has been covered."

— Don't produce more material than can be adequately analysed.

— Pushy/loud group members can dominate the exercise. This will have to be considered in any subsequent discussion, e.g. "Most of the responses seem to have come from ....". Where this can be anticipated the nominal group technique may be the method to use instead.

When to use

The following examples give a good indication of how brainstorming can be used in practice by a team/group to consider:

— What they have done in supervision e.g. "Supervision means to us the following......."

— In planning meetings with councillors. "What we need to get from this meeting is......"

— In creating priority criteria. "Our criteria for determining priorities should be......."

— In creating criteria for admission to a residential unit. "The reasons for admitting children to this unit should be ......"

— Working Party on Reception. "What I want from a receptionist is..........."

— Listing/learning opportunities for young children in a day centre. "To help children learn we need to......."

— Review of duty systems (a) "The Good/Bad News" about our duty system is......." (b)"Our intake system would be improved by......"

— Finding solutions to individual cases. "This client might be helped by........."

Notes and References

1. See, for example, De Bono E. **Lateral Thinking. A Textbook of Creativity** Harmondsworth; Penguin 1977
Rawlinson J.G. **Creative Thinking and Brainstorming** Farnborough: Gower 1981

Brainstorming

43

13. ROLE PLAY

Description

Role play is more commonly used in educational and training contexts to recreate and simulate "real life" situations, and through feedback techniques to develop practice skills. But role play can also by used by work groups as a tool to assess problems and to explore possible solutions in formal supervision, meetings and staff development sessions. Video tapes can be made of the role play to provide feedback and focus discussion. However, arguably more important than video is the feedback given by participants and observers, who can be specially briefed to observe specific aspects of the role-playing process. Additional information and feedback can be obtained by using people as "alter egos" (See E 17 Techniques for giving and receiving feedback to a group).

There are several role play models that can be adapted by work groups for specific purposes. They include:

— Simple approach: This can be used by just two people or by a small group of up to 4 members, where 2/3 act as role players and others observe/act as "alter egos".

— Stop-Start: This is for groups to a maximum of 8-10 people, and incorporates procedures for "stopping" and "re-starting" the action according to a predetermined set of ground rules.

— Serial Role Play: This uses a different procedure to the previous approach, but is designed for a similar size of group.

— Fishbowl: The basic arrangements described in C 10 can also be used for role play purposes.

The role play processes that are common to all forms of role play are described in Fig. 1.

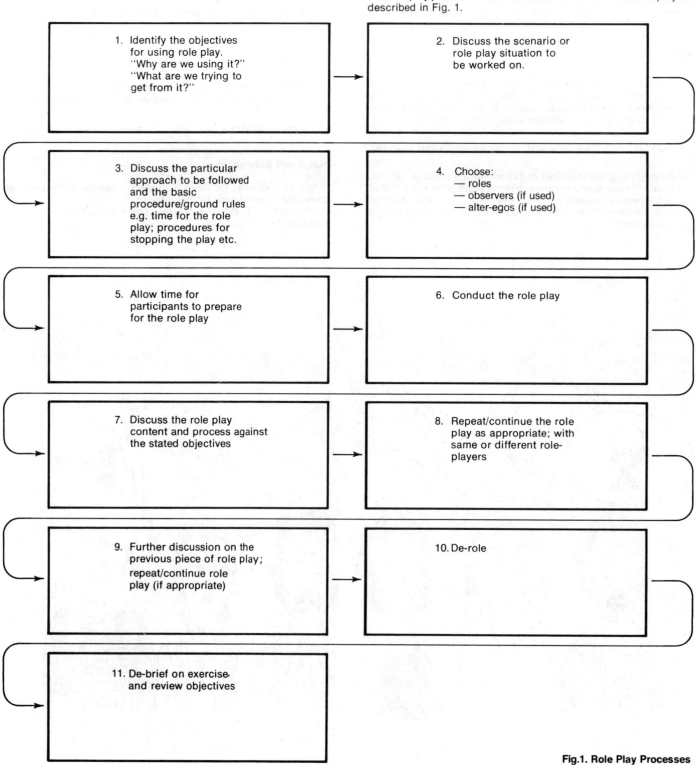

1. Identify the objectives for using role play. "Why are we using it?" "What are we trying to get from it?"

2. Discuss the scenario or role play situation to be worked on.

3. Discuss the particular approach to be followed and the basic procedure/ground rules e.g. time for the role play; procedures for stopping the play etc.

4. Choose:
— roles
— observers (if used)
— alter-egos (if used)

5. Allow time for participants to prepare for the role play

6. Conduct the role play

7. Discuss the role play content and process against the stated objectives

8. Repeat/continue the role play as appropriate; with same or different role-players

9. Further discussion on the previous piece of role play; repeat/continue role play (if appropriate)

10. De-role

11. De-brief on exercise and review objectives

Fig.1. Role Play Processes

Objectives

1. To achieve greater understanding and awareness of a problem/event by re-experiencing it and enabling others to share that experience.

2. To examine a given situation from many viewpoints.

3. To explore some alternative ways of responding to a given problem/situation in relative safety.

4. To allow others to step into one's own shoes so that they can identify with oneself and one's own behaviour.

5. To obtain feedback from others about one's own behaviour and modes of interaction.

Alternative Role-Play Approaches

a) SIMPLE APPROACH (to be used for 2-4 participants)

Procedures

1. Agree roles and focus for the play e.g. the beginning of an interview. Where there are 3 players available, one can act as observer; where there are 4 each player can have an "alter-ego" if the role play is of a one to one encounter

2. Agree time limits and any other rules e.g. for "alter-ego" to intervene, a player to call "stop" if feeling situation out of control, or to play the situation through as a kind of "warm up", discuss and then repeat the process.

3. Allow time (a few minutes is sufficient) for role-players to prepare.

4. Follow procedures as outlined in Fig.1.

When to Use

— This method is useful for individual or small group supervision sessions/training exercises where the content and process of one to one or 3 way discussions are being examined either in prospect, as a rehearsal, or in retrospect to discuss what happened e.g. to role play a recent/future interview with a client or member of some other agency whose help is being sought.

— The method is also useful for role-rehearsal purposes e.g. a player may attempt to take the part of someone whom she/he is actually going to see/has seen.

Simple Approach

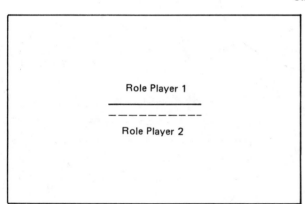

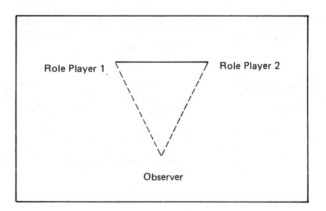

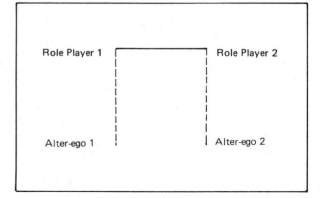

b) STOP-START APPROACH (to be used with small groups of 6-8)

Procedures

1 . The group divides into 2: each side representing one point of view in the ensuing role play. The focus, time limits, "rules" etc. are decided.

2 . One person (or 2 if the situation demands it) is chosen to be the initial role player. The others provide a "support" group to the role player.

3 . Preparations on how to play the role are entered into with each group.

4 . The role play commences. At any point in the action any player/support group member can call "stop" to ask a question, raise a point, make a suggestion or to ask for a brief discussion (like "time out").

5 . The focus is then re-negotiated e.g. a decision may be made to continue the play where it was broken off; to go back to a previous interaction or even to start all over again.

6 . On re-commencement the players may change places with another member of their "support group".

When to Use

— This method is particularly useful for examining confrontational or potentially conflictual situations between individuals/small groups e.g. presenting a proposal for more resources to the Director/Committee.

— It is also useful as a means of engaging all the members of the group in a role play involving a one to one interaction e.g. in a group supervision session, to study an individual member's "case" or problem of relationships with a client/resident.

Stop-Start   Approach

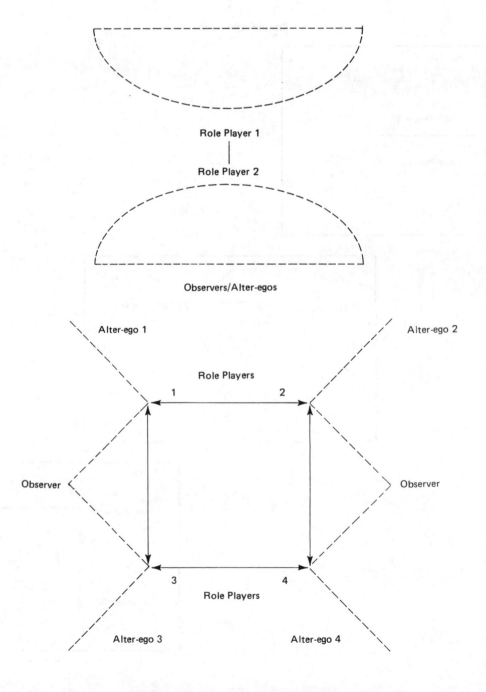

c) SERIAL APPROACH (for use with a small group of 4-6)

Procedures

1. The focus, time limit, ground rules etc. are established as in other approaches.

2. One person is chosen as the "constant" role player (possibly with the help of an "alter ego"). The remainder of the group belong to the "serial" elements.

3. Each member of the "serial" side is given a set time (usually 2-3 minutes) for her/his part in the role play.

4. The role play begins (following preparation time etc) with the first person in the series in interaction with the "constant" player. At the end of the agreed time limit the first player is replaced by the second person in the series, who continues the role play, but usually in her/his own way (thus a variety of responses is provided).

5. The role play ends when all the members of the series have had their turns. De-briefing etc follows.

When to Use

— This method can be used to explore similar situations as in the stop start approach e.g. to present a proposal for more resources to a senior staff member, and a number of tactics can be tried out at different stages of the interview.

Serial Approach

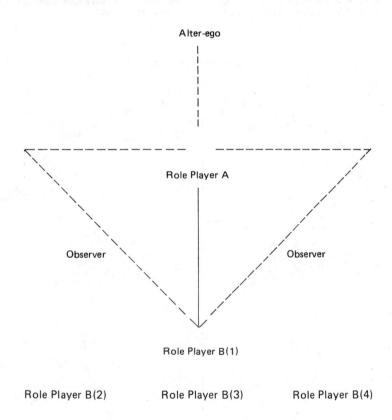

d) FISHBOWL APPROACH (For use with a larger group and where a group role play is the focus)

Procedures

1. The procedures for setting up the fishbowl arrangements are as those described for Closed and Open Fishbowls (See C 10).

2. The role play procedures are as those described in Fig.1.

When to Use

— This method is useful for one group (outer ring) to observe and give feedback on the action of the inner ring, who may be playing a family interview/case conference/review/staff meeting/working party/critical incident or similar group situation.

Do's and Don'ts (For all approaches)

— The intention behind the inclusion of role play in this manual is to encourage its use as a working tool to explore some problems and solutions from alternative perspectives. The more informal the role play process the more likely it is to serve this purpose.

— Do not see it as "play acting" or worry about the dramatical side, but use role play as a method for structuring discussion or parts of one when appropriate. This means that the role play should be brief as a rule, well focussed and directed.

— Choose the most appropriate method to suit the purpose e.g. Fishbowl is more suitable to explore group incidents; Stop-start to examine one to one encounters. Use the Simple method as one would in forming Sub-Groups (C 7) or Buzz Groups (C 8). Here the role plays can be carried out in private as it were and it is the results which get discussed in the wider group.

— Make the role plays short and never more than 10 minutes without a break for discussion; otherwise points get lost. Always allow some time for preparations before beginning a role play, but not too long. Ensure that there is adequate time for discussion after the role play for players will also need to de-role, but this is less of an issue than in the more dramatically intense type of role-play.

Notes and References

For a fuller discussion of role play methods see:
McCaughan N. and Scott T. **Role Play and Simulation Games. Uses in Social Work Education.** National Institute for Social Work Papers No.9 London: NISW 1978.

Douglas R and Payne C. **Five Role Play and Simulation Exercises for Staff in Residential Settings.** London: National Institute For Social Work 1981.

Fishbowl Approach

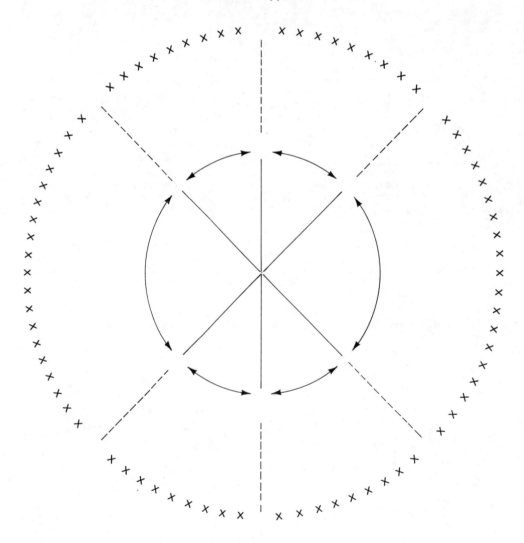

Inner Circle = Role Players

Outer Circle = Observers/Alter-egos

14. SCULPTING

Description

Originating before the Second World War in the work of Moreno and used extensively in family therapy,[1] sculpting techniques can be adapted as a team building and staff development tool. Sculpting makes similar assumptions to other action-learning techniques like role play, psycho-drama and socio-drama. These work on the principle that the creation and re-enactment of inter-personal problems and situations allows expression of feelings, ideas and behaviour through several, rather than a single, modes. This makes learning more insightful and offers greater potential for effecting change in behaviour and relationships.

Sculpting relies almost entirely on non-verbal communication and the expression of body language. One person acting as sculptor attempts to mould or model the behaviour, relationships, patterns of communication that he/she sees in the group. This is done by putting people into various postures and positions that reflect a perceived view of their relationships. Ideally the sculpt should be done silently through gesture and a physical manipulation of the subjects with verbal instructions at a minimum.

Sculpting is usually undertaken with the help of an external consultant, but work groups can learn how to use and apply the techniques without outside help.

Objectives

1. To assess the nature of any problems that might be affecting group relationships.

2. To increase group members' understanding of their own position in relation to others.

3. To increase individuals' understanding of how they might be perceived by others.

4. To initiate changes in behaviour and relationships in a group.

Procedures

1. Preparations: a) It is useful to have some props available; chairs, cushions, tables etc.

   b) It may also be useful to select an observer to record the process of the sculpt.

2. One person volunteers and is chosen to do the initial sculpt.

3. Starting with one member of the group or a sub-group, the sculptor positions her/his material, instructing them with minimum verbal instructions, to adopt the required posture, positions etc.

4. Other member or sub-groups are similarly placed until the whole group is in position. Deliberate use is made of spatial positioning as well as body language.

5. When the tableau is complete the entire group holds itself briefly in a state of tension.

6. Debriefing: Individuals are asked in turn to recall impressions of how they felt in themselves and in relation to one another.

7. Further sculpts may then be attempted.

   a) Comparing current reality with the professed or ideal position. "This appears to indicate how things are in this group; now move to positions where you think you would like them or they ought to be".

   b) Obtaining alternative views. Other members might be asked to make their own sculpt and to adjust the positions to reflect their own perceptions of how things are.

Alternative Method

An alternative but equally effective method for work groups is to ask each person to sculpt her/himself. Posture, attitudes etc will then indicate how each sees him/herself in relation to other individuals and their position in the group as a whole.

Sculpting

Part II — Methods and Techniques

Once everyone has worked out their position the group is asked to remain still for a minute or so before relaxing and entering into discussion on the sculpt and its implications for perceptions, attitudes, relationships etc.

Discussion can be structured by asking each person to think/write down answers to such questions as:

(i)   What I was trying to put across was........

(ii)   What I felt was coming across to me from (a) named individuals (b) the group in general was.......

Further sculpts on the lines of 7(a) and 7(b) above can then be attempted.

Do's and Don'ts

— Do not be surprised if people question the value of doing something like this: they may have a point. Explain the purpose carefully; or encourage people to experiment.

— Note that sculptors do not reflect objective reality; but individual preceptions.

— There should be some basic trust in the group and a willingness to take risks in order for the material developed from sculpts to be used to analyse behaviour and relationships.

— There is always a danger that sculpting may reinforce existing views and attitudes, which are unhelpful to the progress of the group.

— Support may be needed by individuals who are rendered vulnerable by the sculpting, people who are isolated or scapegoated.

When to Use

— A team of workers in a residential unit undertakes a series of sculpting exercises in order to explore and improve their relationships. They use the sculpts to identify their previously unstated concerns about one another's behaviour and relationships in the group.

— A team of social workers uses a series of sculpts to examine the likely impact on roles and relationships of different organisational structures: see Part III (c)

Notes and References

1.   For a useful description of sculpting techniques in work with families see:
     Waldron-Skinner S. Ch.7 "Action techniques" in **Family Therapy** London: Routledge and Kegan Paul, 1976.

15. FLOW CHARTING

Description

There are many ways of displaying visually complex organisational and decision-making processes. Algorithms, critical path analysis and flow charting are some examples of visual representations which guide planning activity and action. They all attempt to identify and map out the key elements or stages in work processes. Flow charts may be used to represent a simple sequence of events.

e.g.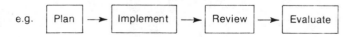

However, organisational processes are usually much more complex so different features and connections between them need to be represented in several ways. In the example[1] provided overleaf the conventions of circles, diagonals, squares are used to represent significant elements in the process, with arrows indicating the flow from one part to another.

Here flow charting is described as a group exercise in order to assist understanding of certain processes and the implications for policies and practice that result.

Objectives

1.   To highlight sequential actions and interrelated processes pictorially or diagramatically.

2.   To assist understanding and analysis of the process involved.

3.   To identify key decision-making points e.g. with a view to reviewing, modifying or monitoring consequent policies and practices.

4.   To provide a guide to organisational policies and practices.

Procedures

1.   Preparations

     a) The group should learn the conventions used.

        In the example given: diamonds = decisions
                                       ◇

                                   squares   actions or
                                   or boxes = events
                                       □

                                   circles   queues or
                                   periods   = waiting
                                       ○   period

     b)   In each ◇ is written the question to be decided. Note this is always phrased to give only two alternative answers, YES/NO.
          (More complex decisions are broken down into sequences of YES/NO questions)

     c)   In each □ is written the Action or Events that occurs.

     d)   In each ○ is written the Queue/Waiting Period that is required.

2.   Designing a Flow Chart

     a)   Form a group around the policy or decision meeting which is being investigated.

     b)   One member of the group is asked to act as a NARRATOR i.e. to describe how she/he thinks the particular policy works in the agency.

     c)   Another member of the group is appointed as RECORDER i.e. to depict the narrator's story in flow chart terms.

     d)   The remainder of the group act as QUESTIONERS controlling the rate and direction of the narration. They have the power to stop the narrator, direct the recorder to back track, move forward, to seek clarification or elaboration on any part of the process and to inject their own ideas. (The

50

Recorder, however, is not usually allowed to question the Narrator.)

e) The Narrator should be given up to 10 minutes private time to collect her/his thoughts.

f) The group will need to decide when the flow chart should begin and end. This is important as it signals the potential size of the task. However, decisions as to the start and end points may change during the analysis.

3. On Completion

On completion of the flow chart the following information should be added:

a) In any one period of time (e.g. week, month, year) write alongside each □ how many clients (or whatever the relevant units are that are, on average, being acted upon); also the minimum and maximum numbers.

b) Using the same time period write alongside each ○ the average and the longest and shortest time clients, or whatever units are being held up, are kept waiting.

c) For each priority decision ◇ indicate whether it is a point at which the flow may be made to go FASTER/SLOWER or provide MORE/LESS service, or to decide to STOP/START a service or whether it is a mixture of two or three of these types.

d) For □, ○ and ◇ write alongside each who is involved in the action, the waiting and the decision making respectively.

4. Review

The group should now review its information display. Some of the questions it may need to consider are:

a) Does the policy fulfil the objectives to be pursued?

b) Are the hold-ups affecting too many people/units, and/or for too long?

c) If hold-ups are a problem how can they be overcome and what are the resource requirements?

d) What changes should be made in either the nature or sequencing of particular decision points?

e) What changes should be made in either the nature or sequencing of particular actions?

f) Will the changes in priority decision points or actions require changes in those who take the decisions or actions?

Do's and Don'ts

— Be prepared to draw and redraw the flow chart several times (e.g. 4/5) in order to achieve a reasonable degree of clarity.

— Ensure that at any one stage in the process, even at the lowest level of detail, all parts of the flow chart from beginning to end are represented. Decisions about which parts of the flow chart to elaborate further can then be taken.

— While continuing the flow chart avoid stating who is involved in the decisions or actions being taken. Concentrate on identifying the questions on which decisions are required and the actions to be taken.

— Ensure that all strings of decisions, actions and queues are drawn to their conclusion (known as the "No Dangles" rule).

— Avoid making the chart too complicated. Start again when this appears to be happening and try to simplify to the key features required.

— Do not become preoccupied with creating a perfect picture. Keep re-drawing to increase accuracy gradually, but do not worry about how it will look. A presentable version can be drawn up on conclusion.

— Ensure that the level of detail used is geared to the reason for doing the analysis, not for the sake of using an interesting technique.

When to Use

— See example of a flow chart overleaf to identify priority decision points for the admission of children to a residential programme.

— Similar examples of referral processes e.g. in an intake team; for admission to a psychiatric hospital under the 1983 Mental Health Act.

— To illustrate key decision making points in a case from referral to closure.

— To develop an action plan for a team or a team policy.

Resources Needed

Large sheets of paper; marker pens. Use different colours to show different features of the process.

Notes and References

1. These procedures and example given are based on an exercise designed by Clive Miller and Tony Scott, when Lecturers in Management at the National Institute, who have given permission for it to be reproduced in this form.

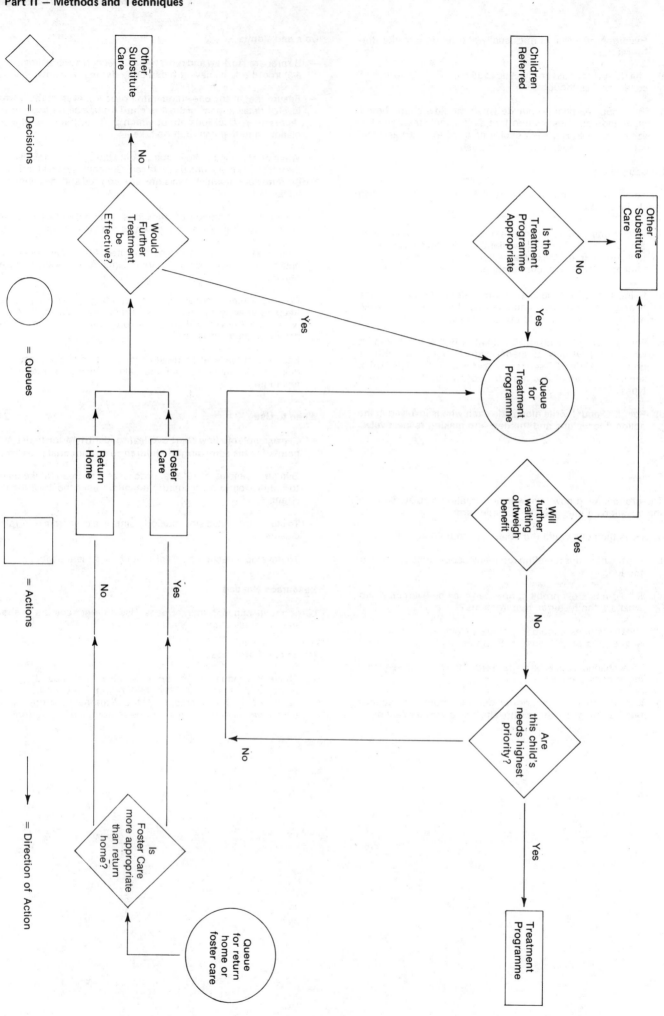

Example: Flow Diagram of Priority Decision Making in Selecting Children into a Residential Home

◇ = Decisions

◯ = Queues

▢ = Actions

→ = Direction of Action

SECTION E   REVIEWING PROGRESS AND PROCESS

Reviewing techniques can be used at the beginning of a meeting to assess members' views about "where they are now" with tasks and their committment to continuing work. Some techniques like "good news/bad news" can also be used as part of the introductions with a new group. They can also be used to take stock of any point during a meeting e.g. at the end of one item before proceeding to the next or at the end of the session.

The techniques described in this section are of two kinds. There are the more general techniques to review progress of task and group process. There are also some specific techniques to provide feedback to a group on its performance.

Contents

16.   Reviewing and Appraisal Techniques   54

17.   Techniques for Giving and Receiving Feedback to a Group   55

16. REVIEWING AND APPRAISAL TECHNIQUES

Description

Reviewing techniques are used to provide group members with some space at the beginning, during or end of a task or meeting to reflect on and convey their personal evaluations of the progress being made with the task and/or of the process. Used at the beginning of a session these techniques can be used to obtain individuals' emotional readiness to start or continue a given task or tasks.

Objectives

1. To review work already started or assess a problem to be begun.

2. To assess commitment, motivation, emotional energy levels etc. of group members to the task in hand.

3. To give every person in a group the opportunity to state their personal views and feelings.

4. To weigh up positives and negatives in order to achieve a balanced view of progress in a given situation.

5. To assist with the planning of the process of the meeting/a particular item.

Some different reviewing techniques are:

a) Good/Bad News
   Each person is asked to state or record a piece of "good/bad" news, which will indicate their views on the progress being made with a given task and/or the process.

b) Regrets and Appreciations
   Individuals are given the opportunity to express one regret and/or appreciation about what they have achieved and/or experienced during the task/session/meeting.

c) Sentence Completion
   "What has helped and/or hindered me to complete the task", or if used at the beginning of a meeting "What has helped and/or hindered me in coming to the meeting today:. . . . .
   Note that appraisal techniques are useful for evaluation at task level and for unloading emotional baggage. (See Part 1, Chapter 2)

Procedures

1. Preparations

   a) Decide on the particular technique or "trigger" to be used. Good/Bad News is a useful general stimulus for both task and process evaluations; though sometimes you may need to specify which type of evaluation is expected.

      Regrets and Appreciations is more commonly used at the end of a session/meeting. "What has helped/hindered" can be adapted for the beginning or end.

   b) Decide whether people should write down evaluations using the Nominal Group Technique (see Section D 11) or simply state what is in their head.

   c) Decide on how long you wish to allocate to the appraisal process.

   d) Decide on a method of recording (if one is used)

2. State ground rules. As a rule each person is allowed one positive and one negative evaluation at any one time e.g. "You are allowed to express one regret and/or one appreciation." People can "pass" if they wish.
   Ask for short statements - particularly if they are to be recorded.

3. Explain the procedures to be followed, e.g. "We go around the room, each person will have an opportunity to speak." or "Write on the card provided your good/bad news," "Call out any pieces of good/bad news as you think of them - they will be recorded on the flip chart" etc.

4. Allow time at the end to discuss further any important statements that have been made and for general impressions to be summarised and aired.

5. Follow up. You will need to consider how information is to be used/processed.

6. To record information

   a) People can pin written evaluations on the wall/board; followed by informal discussion and possibly further more formal discussion on the material.

   b) A recorder can be appointed to write down verbal/written statements under the respective headings.

   c) People may need to be supplied with writing paper, ink or cans of poster paint to mount an "art gallery" (See H 22).

   d) Individuals might be asked to write their evaluations direct on to a flip chart, poster, black/white board, overhead projector etc.

Do's and Don'ts

— Avoid being overwhelmed by information. This can be done by limiting contributions to one positive and/or negative statement per person.

— Do not use the exercise as a substitute for a more rigorous and systematic evaluation procedure, though it may act as a stimulus for one.

— Encourage as many people as possible to participate in the exercise. Try and identify the positives where they exist.

— Consider carefully whether you need verbal only and/or written evaluations/recorded statements. Much will depend on why you need the information.

When to Use

— Within a team meeting to obtain some brief evaluation of current working practices e.g. "Let's find out the good/bad news about our recording methods/staff meeting/team atmosphere/climate" etc.

— To begin and/or end staff meetings/supervision sessions/training sessions: "What has helped/hindered me in coming here today.........", "An appreciation/regret about today has been ....".

"Good" News	"Bad" News
Useful for supervision purposes Able to dicate notes	Records not kept up to date Long-winded

Examples of "Good/Bad" News about recording and methods.

17. TECHNIQUES FOR GIVING AND RECEIVING FEEDBACK TO A GROUP

a) Observers

b) Alter-egos

c) Audio/Video Tapes

Objectives

1. To enable a group of individuals within a group to review, evaluate and change their ways of working.

2. To provide feedback and support to key people.

3. To assist people's learning of group processes and behaviour.

4. To provide analysis of what is currently being experienced in a group.

5. To provide ways of handling specific interactional and performance problems.

a) Observers

One way of obtaining feedback for a group is by asking one person(s) to withdraw from the discussion and act as an observer. Observations can be made of the group process and/or of the behaviour and performance of individual members. This enables the group to review and evaluate its progress. Observers need a clear brief. An agreement should be made with the group about how the information is to be used.

Observers

Alter-egos

b) Alter-egos

"Alter-ego" means "other self" and is a device used frequently in role play to provide the actors, notably the leading characters, with a second voice and as a source of support. The alter-ego principle can be used in live work to provide feedback to individuals on their behaviour or even to intervene and demonstrate alternative ways of responding as the action takes place. For example, the "alter" ego stands behind the "ego" and when "alter" wishes to participate puts a hand on "ego's" shoulder. "Ego" stops and allows "alter" to take his/her place. When "alter" finishes she/he takes the hand from "ego's" shoulder and "ego" continues as before.

As with observers, using alter-egos requires specific agreements about the purpose, limits and procedures to be followed.

c) Use of Audio/Video Tapes

Feedback can also be obtained by making an audio or video tape of a meeting. Tapes have the advantage of giving feedback direct to the individuals or group concerned instead of using a third party as with observers.

The technical preparations and procedures are described in Section H on Using Audio/Visual Aids. As with observers it is important the group know how it will use the tapes to learn from them and to change their behaviour subsequently. Agreements about how the tapes are to be used and access to them are needed. Additional time for viewing or listening to the tapes is needed. When viewing/listening it is useful to have some briefing questions to focus attention and to make selective use of the material.

Do's and Don'ts

— All three techniques require a relatively high level of trust to be present in the group.

— It is important to establish explicit agreements or "contracts" amongst group members on a number of points:

- the reasons for seeking and providing feedback

- the specific goals for any particular piece of feedback

- boundaries i.e. what is permissible to give feedback on and what is "out of court".

- the limits to which any information so gained will be used i.e. whether it is to be used only in and by the group. (See also Part 1 Chapter 2)

— It is useful for observers to be given briefing sheets, which provide them with a focus and boundaries. The questions can be developed in consultation with the group so forming a kind of "contract". Similarly a group can develop its own briefing sheet for use when listening to/viewing tapes.

When to Use

— Observers and/or audio/video tapes can be used whenever a work group wants to review its own working processes so that it can learn from the feedback and improve its performance, e.g. in a team development exercise observers give feedback.

— Alter-egos is a more specialised approach to be used where an individual is seeking help over some aspects of his/her performance and reaches an agreement to be given some "live" feedback, e.g. a group member who seeks to improve his/her skills as chairperson/group leader.

— In training sessions involving role play alter-egos can be used in a variety of ways (See D13).

Television

SECTION F   TAKING DECISIONS BY VOTING

Voting procedures, though not infallible, are useful for work groups to take decisions which obtain majority or consensus support. At the least they ensure that the degree of support for any particular proposal or point of view is made public. Voting procedures are commonly used to obtain agreements on the outcome of a piece of work, particularly where further action is to be taken. However, they may also be used under some circumstances to obtain agreements on the methods or processes to be used by the group.

Contents

18. How To Use Voting Procedures   60

18. HOW TO USE VOTING PROCEDURES

Description

Voting procedures, though not infallible, are useful to enable work groups to take decisions, which command majority or consensus support. At least they ensure that the degree of support for any particular proposal or point of view is made public. Voting procedures are commonly used to obtain agreements on the outcome of a piece of work, particularly where further action is to be taken. However, they may also be used under some circumstances to obtain agreements on the methods or processes which can determine the options or choices open to group members in the final count.

Procedures can be classified on a continuum from Simple to Complex. For most purposes work groups will probably prefer the simpler voting procedure; where the issues at choice are more complex, more sophisticated procedures may be adopted. (See below)

Simple	Complex
Definition	
FIRST PAST THE POST	ABSOLUTE MAJORITY SECURES
i.e. proposal registering most support is accepted, regardless of combined strength of alternatives.	i.e. for any proposal to be accepted it must register over 50% of the votes cast.
Methods	If absolute majority not obtained on first ballot and the least favoured proposal is eliminated another ballot is held. Votes are then transferred from the other proposals.
Public show of hands; secret ballot; where several choices are available a "preference" system may be adopted. Votes are cast in order of preference and each choice "weighted" to yield an overall score.	The process continues with as many ballots and eliminations as are needed to obtain the absolute majority.

Objectives

1. To ensure that the decisions which have been taken by a work group, i.e. about its working methods and processes and future action, command a strong measure of support.

2. To ensure accountability and responsibility in group decision taking.

3. To involve each group member minimally in the decision taking process.

4. To provide a fair means by which roles and tasks can be allocated within a group.

Procedures

Preparations: for a simple show of hands no preparations are required, apart from the appointment of tellers.

— If a secret ballot is being used, voting slips and ballot boxes will have to be prepared; also the means of ensuring confidentiality will have to be devised e.g. by appointing independent tellers.

— More complex procedures will require more attention to preparation e.g. determination of weighting systems; methods of calculations etc.

Do's and Don'ts

— Try to ensure that the appropriate system is used for particular circumstances. Use the simplest method possible.

— Voting systems can mask real differences of opinion that continue long after the vote has been taken. Do not see a vote as an ultimate solution.

— Ensure that voters understand the processes they are engaging in, i.e. they know what they are voting for and why.

— Voters will also need to understand the implications of what they are voting for in terms of its consequences. Decisions can often be rendered impotent by lack of action afterwards.

— The timing of the vote is critical. It must not be taken too quickly before all the arguments or proposals have been heard; neither should "filibustering" be allowed to ruin the process.

— Note that a low turnout may make the outcome of the vote open to dispute.

When To Use

Voting procedures can be used:

— at the beginning of a meeting e.g. to obtain agreements on working methods and content.

— at the end of a task or piece of work to determine future action.

— as part of the work process, to take stock and determine subsequent courses of action and procedures which lead to the final outcome or decision taking.

Examples of Use

— In Agenda Setting
Voting procedures may be used to establish an agenda for a meeting, where there is no concensus or shared assumptions about the purposes or content, e.g. votes can be cast to determine the number of agenda items, which might be considered and their order of priority.

— In Group Formation
Members can vote to join a particular group/sub group by stating their preferences according to some agreed criteria.

— In Work Allocation
In taking decisons over how work tasks should be allocated or undertaken or who might be the most appropriate person(s) to undertake a particular piece of work.

— In Nominal Group Work (See D 11)
Where a number of alternative proposals/solutions have been put forward and a decision is needed on which idea appears to be the most favoured.

SECTION G   ENDINGS

The ending of a group, like joining and starting, involves people in a number of transitional processes. These may include:

— reviewing the progress made by the group in relation to its stated objectives

— reviewing the process of belonging to a group at the personal and emotional level

— looking ahead to the application of ideas and contexts from the group experience in other work situations

— loss of roles and status acquired in the group

— developing the means by which contacts formed in the group can be continued in the future, when, if desired and if appropriate.

The techniques described in this section are all designed to assist different aspects of the ending process. They can be used separately or in conjunction with one another according to the particular needs and circumstances. They can also be used in conjunction with the reviewing techniques described in Section E.

Contents

19.   Drawing Shields   62

20.   The Cocktail Party   63

21.   Guided Phantasy   64

22.   Action Planning   65

23.   Forming Networks   67

19. DRAWING SHIELDS

Description

A visual means of reviewing and evaluating the group experience. The display of shields in an "art gallery" provides an opportunity for the public expression and sharing of individuals' feelings about the ending of the group.

Objectives

1. To complete and record in visual form a personal evaluation of the group experience.

2. To compare one's own perception of the group with that of others by receiving feedback from them.

3. To give feedback to others as a piece of self evaluation.

Procedures

1. Each person is given a large sheet of drawing paper and access to coloured pens/pencils.

2. Explain that the task is for each to convey their feelings about leaving the group by drawing a shield: an emblem of their group experience.

3. The shield is divided into 3 sections. Each shield should depict:

   a) The happiest and most pleasurable experience in the group.

   b) The most frustrating experience.

   c) Where one will be in a year's time.

   d) An epitaph or a motto.

4. The shields are drawn and displayed in an "art gallery" with some informal discussion in small groups to enlarge comments.

Do's and Don'ts

— This type of exercise is effective with groups who are already committed to expressing themselves in these ways. It can't be sprung on a group that is unaccustomed to more unconventional ways of working.

— This kind of evaluation is limited to the expressive elements of the group experience and usually will need to be supplemented by other approaches.

— Some people may be reluctant to participate because of inhibitions about their artisitic abilities. Explain that the object is not to display artistic talents; even very crude symbols and drawings can effectively meet the purpose of the exercise.

When To Use

— The final session of a training course.

— The final session of a work group that has been in existence for some time.

Note

Shields can also be drawn at the beginning of an event, where they can be used to express participants hopes, fears, aspirations, personal goals and expectations etc.

BEFORE

AFTER

Drawing Shields

20. THE COCKTAIL PARTY

Description

As the title suggests the cocktail party is a social event that gives group members an opportunity to state any unfinished business they may have in relation to other individual or sectional interests. The "cocktails" take the form of pieces of fruit, often bananas which serve as symbols of food and drink.

Objectives

1. To develop a relaxed atmosphere in which some important statements can be made by participants.

2. To allow individuals to offload any emotional luggage about the group before they leave.

3. To allow for the completion of any unfinished business between members of the group.

4. To facilitate the formation of support networks which will operate after the group has formally ended.

Procedures

Preparations

1. To convey an air of novelty and surprise about the final meeting ask group members to bring a piece of fruit, an apple, banana, small bunch of grapes etc.

2. Pile all these contributions on a plate at the beginning of the meeting.

The "Cocktail Party"

3. Explain that the final part of the meeting (eg. 15 - 20 minutes from the end) will be spent informally with members circulating freely.

4. Explain also that there is a purpose and task e.g. to enable people to say to one another what otherwise might be left unsaid. In this way boundaries can be drawn around the group.

5. Offer the cocktails and encourage people to interact for the duration before the group or event is formally brought to an end.

Do's and Don'ts

— Ensure that the group members have a clear idea of the task: that it is not intended as a piece of social chit-chat.

When To Use

— The final session of a group that has been in existence for some time.

— The final session of a training course.

Cocktail Party

21. GUIDED PHANTASY

Description

A technique derived from psychotherapy to facilitate the transition from one situation to another and to anticipate future experiences, which might cause pain or stress.

In working contexts it can be used as a role-rehearsal technique, helping people to anticipate and feel through a future event. A narrator or prompter is used to provide a range of cues that stimulate the imagination and awareness of the situation which is being entered into.

Objectives

1. To assist process of leaving, entry and re-entry.

2. To provide an opportunity to anticipate and rehearse, mentally and emotionally, some future event.

3. To identify and consider how to manage some of the stresses and anxieties that accompany changes of situation.

Procedures

1. One person is chosen as narrator or prompter. She/he may need to prepare a short story or cue questions that guide the phantasy.

2. Participants are encouraged to take up a relaxed position by shutting their eyes, lying down etc. so that they can empty their minds of current preoccupations.

3. The guided phantasy begins. The narrator can tell a story, eg:

"Once upon a time, there was a group of people who . . . . . .
When they left they had to . . . .
When they returned to their offices they . . . ."
thereby stimulating people to think of themselves in that kind of situation. One can ask a series of questions which are related to different parts of the process e.g. "What are you likely to see, hear, smell, touch as you enter the office on your return?", "What will you say to them?", "What are they likely to say to you?", "What will be the first thing you will do on starting work?"

4. After the narrator has finished participants, if they wish, can discuss their thoughts and feelings; or they might write down their impressions so that they can check later how far their phantasies match up to the impending reality.

Do's and Don'ts

— It is important that there should be a relaxed and trusting atmosphere.

— Make sure that the narrator is given sufficient time to prepare.

— Ensure that people are seated comfortably; cushions might be supplied if people wish to lie on the floor.

— Make sure that the narration does not go on too long; 5-10 minutes will be enough.

— Allow plenty of time afterwards for the experience to be worked through as powerful emotions can be aroused.

When To Use

— At the end of an away day to sort out office problems, so that individuals and/or group can focus on the return to normal working patterns or relationships.

— At the end of a training programme for individuals to anticipate their return to work.

— During an individual/group supervision session to rehearse some future situation e.g. interview with a client which is causing anxiety.

— The technique can also be used in practice with clients e.g. helping someone mourn by re-living a funeral or by encouraging a young person to think about a job interview.

— As an insight-giving technique e.g. on an induction course to help new residential workers imagine how residents feel when they come into care.

Guided Phantasy

22. ACTION PLANNING

Description

Action planning refers to a process often used at the end of training courses to encourage students to apply their learning. Similar processes can be used by work groups to formulate plans of action and develop the means by which future activities can be reviewed and evaluated.

Frameworks to focus planning can be devised; the example given overleaf is an adaptiation of something called a "change planner". This encourages the users to identify and set realistic objectives and targets, to consider the means by which they can be attained and any difficulties that can be anticipated.

Objectives

1. To encourage detailed thinking about how ideas can be implemented.

2. To develop a realistic and practical plan of action.

3. To provide the means by which future activities can be reviewed and evaluated.

4. To encourage the members of a group to continue their thinking and learning after the completion of their work together.

Procedures

1. The action planner is given out and time given for individuals to complete it. Encourage people to work privately to begin with i.e. following the rule of the Nominal Group Technique (See D11).

2. The subsequent stages can use any of the group techniques described elsewhere in this section, i.e. form sub-groups; a group chaining; fishbowl discussions etc., to exchange ideas and receive feedback.

   Action plans can also be displayed in an "Art Gallery" (See H 24)

(The particular techniques used will depend on the purposes and outcomes sought).

3. Arrangements can be made to review the success of the action plans after a period of implementation.

Do's and Don'ts

— Allow sufficient time for individuals to complete all the sections of the plan before entering into discussion.

— Encourage people to set realistic and attainable targets. Targets should be described in ways that will enable people to know if they have reached them or not i.e. in specific terms of the actions that will have to be taken to reach a destined goal.

   eg. "to negotiate group supervision session with the team once a fortnight; the sessions to run over a 6 month period before being evaluated".

— Similarly the tasks and activities needed to attain goals should be made as specific as possible.

   eg. "to interview every potential group member for about half an hour, in order to ascertain views about the value of group supervision; then to report the results at a group meeting. The interview schedule is to be completed by the end of the month."

— Encourage people to use their action plan as a tool for reviewing progress and performance.

When To Use

— At the end of a course/training exercise/workshop particularly one where ideas for change and development are under consideration.

— As a group exercise to indicate how a project or proposal might be implemented with individuals undertaking different tasks.

Example: Action Planner   (The following statements can be used as a basic framework. Simplify or modify as appropriate).

Action Planner

1. Statement of change being sought:

   "One change/improvement that I would like to see implemented

   is . . . ."

2. Identify specific goals/targets:

   "For this improvement to be made the following targets/goals need to be attained:

   a) . . . .

   b) . . . .

   c) . . . ."

3. Actions in relation to goals:

   "The actions/steps needed to attain each goal are:

   a) . . . .

   b) . . . .

   c) . . . ."

4. Using opportunities and resources:

   a) "The opportunities/available resources which I can

   use (for each goal) are . . . ."

   b) "The most effective way of using such opportunities

   are likely to be . . . ."

5. Anticipating obstacles/difficulties:

   a) "The obstacles/hindrances to reaching my goals are

   likely to be . . . ."

   b) "I might overcome these obstacles by . . . ."

6. People:

   a) "The key people who I might have to influence are

   . . . ."

   b) "The people who I can rely on to help me with my

   plans are . . . ."

7. Time-Scale:

   "What activities (in relation to each goal) can I realisitically undertake by the end of:

   One week . . . .

   One month . . . .

   Three months . . . ."

8. Review and Evaluation:

   "To evaluate progress I intend to use the following methods . . ."

---

23. FORMING NETWORKS

Description

The means by which links can be established with people holding a common interest relating to a project, task or exercise and who are prepared to maintain contact with one another. Contacts can be maintained by meetings, correspondence and telephone.

Objectives

1. To develop the means by which support and advice can be obtained by people with common interests and work problems.

2. To provide a continuous teaching and learning resource by people offering their knowledge and skills to one another.

3. To continue relationships that have been formed under particular circumstances e.g. a training course, work group.

Procedures

1. A network can be formed by a group of people exchanging:

   — addresses

   — telephone numbers

   — common interests

   — information needs

   — knowledge of resources

2. An agreement needs to be made by members of the network over:

   — how they might maintain contact with one another e.g. by correspondence, telephone, occasional meetings

   — the kind of things which people may need and/or offer one another e.g. information, support, sharing of new knowledge and ideas.

3. Where meetings are planned it is important to decide:

   — who should organise and co-ordinate them

   — how often they should be held

   — what should be their content and focus

Do's and Don'ts

— Ensure that any arrangements are feasible and practical; do not in the first flush of enthusiasm bite off more than you can chew.

— Collect as much of the necessary information when potential members are present and available; do not rely on promises of the "I'll do it next week" variety. To maintain interest the benefits need to be quickly apparent.

— Decide whether the network should be open-ended, running the risk of dying a natural death; or time-limited. Agreements about continuation should be re-negotiated from time to time.

— Try to record and circulate all the relevant information as quickly as possible to members after the network has been formed. Build in the means by which information can be brought up to date.

— Try to share out tasks; don't leave one person to do all the work. Commitment is not maintained in this way.

— Ensure that any meetings are carefully planned and structured. Prevent the feelings,"why are we here"; "This is a waste of time".

— Avoid entering into arrangements without considering carefully the likely benefits and commitment involved. Do not form the network for sentimental reasons only, or because a group is unable to face the reality of ending.

When to Use

Any work group that sees itself as having something in common can agree to form itself into a network - when there is a clear and mutually agreed purpose.

e.g. — to continue work begun on a training course

   — a group initially put in touch with one another because it is known that members have common interests and knowledge

   — a group working on a particular project/task who agree to keep one another informed between sessions.

SECTION H   USING AUDIO/VISUAL AIDS

How information is fed into and dealt with by a group is important in terms of using time efficiently and for sustaining interest and commitment. A group that is unable to take in information, forgets most of what is being discussed, or becomes bored because of lack of variety in the way it works, is unlikely to obtain the best possible results.

There are many aids, some simple, others more sophisticated, which can be used to present and record information. The use of these aids increases the prospects of maintaining involvement and participation at the level required for effective performance.

Contents

24. Art Gallery   70

25. Presenting and Displaying Information   71

26. Using Tapes and Slides   76
    (Audio tapes; video tapes; tape-slide sets; films)

24. ART GALLERY

Description

A specific type of visual display where group members display their contributions, usually on sheets of paper, on walls or boards. This approach is particularly useful for teams to display work after a normal group technique, buzz groups and work done in sub-groups. (See C and D).

Objectives

1. To allow groups to share work of individual or sub groups

2. To summarise and record ideas and information for later use.

3. To encourage group ownership of material.

Procedures

1. Allocate material (paper and marker pens) to groups preparing their display.

2. Ask the group to record work on the sheets of paper as per instructions.

3. On completion, arrange the large sheets around the walls of the main group room or on display boards.

4. Allow time for group members to view the assembled Art Gallery and to discuss the contents.

5. Collect and store material for further use and typing up if needed.

Do's and Don'ts

— Ensure that sheets have names on them, are headed and numbered, particularly if they are to be typed up and to be discussed at a later stage.

— Make sure there is an adequate supply of large sheets of paper and pens; spare pens are always needed.

— Remember to prepare a wall/display space and the means of sticking the papers up e.g. by blue tac/drawing pins.

— Ensure that the group is clear about the task and what is to be recorded.

— Allow sufficient time for viewing and discussion.

— Too much information can be difficult to absorb, so encourage concise recording and clear presentations.

— The material may need to be typed up, edited, duplicated and distributed. Allow sufficient time to organise these tasks.

— Have any such material typed and edited as soon as possible. After its production it quickly loses its meaning, particularly when originally in note form.

When To Use

Examples:

— To record the views of sub-groups about proposed organisational changes.

— To present the results of a piece of nominal work i.e. individuals writing up responses on large sheets and displaying them round the room.

— To present information from the different stages of a group project.

Art Gallery

25. PRESENTING AND DISPLAYING INFORMATION

Description

The use of a:

— blackboard

— whiteboard

— overhead projector

— flip chart or posters

can assist the presentation of information needed by a group; such aids can also be used to record or display ideas developed during a meeting.

Objectives

1. To ensure that information and ideas are presented clearly and received by a wide audience.

2. To keep a public record of information and ideas, which are being presented or discussed.

3. To receive ideas or feedback from members of a group.

4. To encourage group members to contribute their ideas and make them public.

5. To encourage group members to clarify issues and to achieve a more focussed discussion.

6. To maintain interest and commitment to the group task.

Presenting Information

1. Preparation

a) Choose the most appropriate format for the purpose; e.g. blackboard, white board, overhead projector, flip board etc.

b) Select key ideas - avoid presenting too much material. Prepare diagrams, tables etc as appropriate.

c) If using an overhead projector or flip board limit the number of items on any one sheet/plate.

d) Use different colours to underline and to emphasise specific points.

e) Keep material covered up (e.g. with a sheet of paper) until ready to be presented (to make sure the audience is not distracted or focussing on the incorrect information).

f) Check that plates/sheets are in correct sequence.

g) Check that any equipment is in good working order; also that there is an adequate supply of materials e.g. pens, more blank plates/sheets of paper.

2. Presentation

a) Ensure that the audience can read the material and that seating arrangements are appropriate.

b) Allow sufficient time for the ideas to be absorbed and opportunities for questions.

c) Try to pace the presentation so that each part is given the appropriate amount of time and consideration.

d) Speak facing the audience wherever possible (more difficult when blackboard/whiteboard being used.)

Displaying Information

When To Use

Examples

— To present proposals about making changes to policies and procedures.

— To present agendas for a meeting

— To present material at a staff training/supervision session

Using Visual Aids to Assist Group Participation and Discussion

1. A board, flip charts etc. should be made so that views, ideas can be set down and displayed during a discussion by any member of the group.

2. Some people may be reluctant initially to present their ideas in such a public way, but with encouragement can do so in ways that are helpful to the group.

3. As for any other purpose equipment needs to be in good working order and an adequate supply of pens etc available.

4. The equipment needs to be positioned so that it is easily accessible by potential contributors.

When To Use

Examples

— To form an agenda at the beginning of a meeting

— To enable a group member clarify or elablorate an idea or proposal

— To assist in processes of listing, clustering etc (see I 30)

Recording Information

1. Preparation

   a) Ensure that an adequate supply of blank paper, acetate sheets etc. is available.

2. Recording

   a) Allow time to get the points down; don't rush if it means the writing will be illegible.

   b) Print/write in large, bold hand; avoid cramping points.

   c) Concentrate on taking down key points/phrases (unless verbatim recording is required as in brainstorming and nominal group technique).

   d) Check on accuracy and adequacy of statements being recorded.

   e) Ascertain what should be done with the material on completion e.g. is it to be kept? typed up? how confidential should it be?

When To Use

Examples

— To record discussion points in meetings, supervision sessions etc.

— To obtain ideas for discussion/agenda building.

— To record results of brainstorming, nominal group technique, buzz groups etc.

Using Different Formats: Advantages and Disadvantages

The main formats, which can be used to present and record information:

— blackboard

— whiteboard

— overhead projector

— flipchart

— poster paper (printers offcuts, butcher's paper etc)

have certain advantages and disadvantages in terms of:

— costs

— availability/accessibility

— flexibility of use

— effectiveness

— ease of use

These are summarised in Fig.1.

Fig. 1. Formats: advantages and disadvantages

	Blackboard	Whiteboard	Overhead Projector	Flip Chart	Poster Paper
Characteristics	Fixed/portable	Fixed/portable	Several models available including portable	Portable (but tends to be cumbersome)	Comes in sheets/rolls
Materials Needed	Chalk (white colours) Use non dust chalk where possible.	Marker pens. Wet/dry depending on permanent/water based type.	Requires screen/light wall, acetate sheets/rolls, special pens (permanent/water).	Easel/stand. Pads of paper, marker pens.	Marker pens, blue tac, tape, drawing pin to stick on walls
Cleaning	Rubber, cloth (wet/dry)	Permanent - need special cleaning fluid. Water based -wet/dry cloth	Electricity, sockets, plugs and extension leads Permanent –special cleaning fluid Water - wet cloth	Paper can be stored/discarded after use.	Sheets can be stored/discarded after use

Fig. 1. Continued.

Format	Costs	Accessibility/ Availability	Flexibility	Effectiveness	Ease of use
Blackboard	Capital: Requires high initial outlay Running: Chalk supplies reasonably cheap, also dusters	Occupies a relatively small area on a wall /corner of room if portable. Chalk etc easily obtained.	Fixed location a drawback; portable black-boards often difficult to move about	Fixed space limits the content, and variety limited by choice of colours. Material difficult to retain. Presenter usually has to write with back to audience Strong associations with school may be unhelpful	Chalk tends to be dusty and quickly runs out
Whiteboard	Capital: Requires an initial outlay, which can be quite high. Running: more expensive than blackboard. Requires special pens ("wet" or "dry") and special cleaning material (depending on type)	As above	As above	As above	Special markers required for different types of board; also markers may be permanent ink requiring special cleansing fluid. Make sure board and markers match.
Overhead Projector	Most expensive of the formats in terms of initial outlay and running costs. Special acetate plates/ rolls and pens are required; also replacement lamps	Small and can be easily stored away; requires electric sockets correct plugs etc also screen/white wall space	Is fairly portable (providing sockets available); acetate plates can be stored and carried around; screen has to be correctly positioned	Variety of formats and presentations possible. Has advantage that material can be retained if needed. Content restricted only by the amount of roll/number of plates.Presenter able to face audience. Room may have to be darkened during use therefore causing some people to drop off.	Pens may use permanent/non permanent ink. Special cleansing fluid required for former. Requires technical expertise in setting up and making adjustments; also to replace burned out lamps possibly.

Fig. 1. Continued.

Format	Costs	Accessibility/ Availability	Flexibility	Effectiveness	Ease of Use
Flip Chart/Pad	Easel can be quite expensive; also pads tend to consist of higher quality/more expensive paper. Constant supply of marker pens needed.	Easily stored; pads can be used without the easel if necessary. Obtainable from office suppliers.	Good portability, easel folds away in boot of car; needs good position in room to be seen by everyone.	Material can be permanent and presented on a number of sheets and "flipped" over. Choice of colours can be wide. Only one or two people can use it at a time.	Flip chart easel may be heavy and difficult to adjust. Problems sometimes finding unused sheets in a pad.
Poster paper i.e. Printers Offcuts or Butchers Paper.	Cheapest in terms of outlay and running costs. Requires constant supply of marker pens and blue-tac, tape, drawing pins to stick on walls/ boards.	Material easily obtained from printers/office supplies. Can be used as roll/ pre-cut sheets	Very portable; paper can be carried around in rolls/ holders. Can be used wherever there is appropriate wall space.	Cheap paper can look amateurish. Has all the advantages of a flip-chart; but sheets need to be spread out over a wall. This can some-times lead to too much information being displayed at a time. Sheets not in use can be covered up however.	Sheets can be used and discarded at will. Sometimes a problem in finding adequate wall space, walls where blue tac is allowed. Easily becomes tatty.

26. USING TAPES AND SLIDES
(Audio tapes, video tapes, tape/slide sets, films etc)

Description

Some kinds of information can be presented using tapes/slides to supplement or complement the spoken word. This can also stimulate analysis and discussion. Tapes can also be made by work groups for their own internal purposes (See for example E17, Techniques for Giving and Receiving Feedback to a Group) and for the purposes of disseminating information to others.

As in H 25 Fig. 1, the different modes (Audio tapes etc) have their advantages and disadvantages for different purposes. In general terms each can be evaluated for its:

- flexibility;
- range of application and use;
- costs;
- technical complexity;
- time needed for preparation, transport, storage etc.

Using Prepared Tapes/Films/Slides

Objectives

1. To provide specific information and ideas via an alternative medium to talking.

2. To provide a trigger or stimulus to other work.

3. To provide the basis for discussion/investigation of issues.

4. To provide a stimulating alternative or addition to other methods of presentation.

Procedures

1. Preparation

   a) Select the mode of presentation which is appropriate to your purpose, i.e. film, tape, slides.

   b) Ensure that you have all the equipment needed e.g. projector, leads and sockets, film, screen etc.

   c) Ensure that the equipment is compatible - a VHS video tape needs a VHS VCR.

   d) Make certain that the equipment is in good working order before use - always test it out and have a trial run (particularly if films/tapes are being hired - they might be of poor quality/ worn).

   e) Organise time and place - remember privacy and quiet may be needed. Prepare the room in advance. Don't leave these preparations until the last minute.

   f) Remember to order any tapes/slides well in advance.

2. Presentation

   a) Prepare viewers; often a key sentence is useful, such as "The most helpful thing Mr. X did was ...." or "The key problem was......."

   b) Explain length and nature of presentation.

   c) Indicate when questions can be asked and how much discussion time is available.

3. Discussion

   Allow sufficient time for discussion after the presentation, usually at least as long as the presentation itself.

When To Use

- Tape (audio/visual) can be used to obtain feedback on a group or individual's performance in staff meeting, supervision sessions etc.

- Such material can be developed to assess current performance and then stored for later use in order to evaluate progress at a later date.

- To develop material that will inform others of a project in which group members are involved.

Do's and Don'ts

- Watch for equipment that fails or is incompatible with the tapes/ slides (particularly so in video tapes).

- Ensure sufficient time to analyse and discuss material.

- Ensure that there is sufficient preparation for people making visual/audio aids; an amateur performance may be a giggle but it can also be irritating and counter-productive.

- Be clear about reasons for using tapes etc.; it may sometimes be more important to talk than view.

- People perceive/hear very different things from audio/visual sources; making it difficult to ensure the goals are met.

- Check that the follow up discussion is focussed.

- Tapes and slides can only show SNAPSHOTS of reality; video tapes are better but still can distort problems.

Video

SECTION I   FOCUSSING AND STRUCTURING TECHNIQUES

These are all tools which encourage participation in the work process by structuring and focussing attention on specific issues. They can be used for a variety of purposes and by different group arrangements. Some, e.g. briefing notes, have been referred to in other sections of the manual. All such tools are used to make efficient use of time and energy and to achieve more effective outcomes.

Contents

27. Trigger Sentences   80

28. Briefing Notes and Handouts   80

29. Planning Frameworks   81

30. Listing and Clustering   87

31. Using Pattern Recording Techniques   88

27. TRIGGER TECHNIQUES

Description

There are many techniques that can be used to cue or prompt discussion and working on given tasks. We call these trigger techniques because they "trigger" thought and action on a set path; thus helping to focus and structure the discussion or work. The most commonly used are trigger sentences. Visual cues (pictures, drawings, video clips) can serve a similar purpose in some contexts.

A trigger sentence usually consists of the beginning of a sentence, which then has to be completed and expanded, as the task demands.

Objectives

1. To provide a way of sparking off thinking or discussion.

2. To help focus thinking on a given topic or subject.

3. To obtain a number of different statements but on a common theme.

Procedures

1. Trigger sentences can be issued verbally or in writing e.g. on blackboard or as part of a questionaire e.g. the Personal Disclosure Checklist (B 6), whenever needed to prompt or stimulate a response.

2. State or write out the trigger as appropriate. (See below for examples).

Do's and Don'ts

— Keep the trigger brief and simple e.g. "What I expect from this meeting is........"

— Choose when to use triggers carefully, otherwise they can appear rather artificial.

— Watch out for members who use the trigger in silly or destructive, and other inappropriate ways.

When To Use

Triggers can be used with many of the other techniques described in this manual at the beginning, during or at the end of meetings.

Examples in Use

Setting an Agenda (A3: "What we need to work on today is.......")

Using a Personal Disclosure Checklist (B6: "What I want this group to achieve is......")

Starting off a Fishbowl (C10: "What I have heard today is.......")

Nominal Group Technique (D11: Everyone writes out "Three things I want to know about are.....")

Brainstorming (D12: "Our record system could be improved by.......")

To start off a role-play (D13: "Mrs Smith says to you......)

To discuss the results of sculpt (D14: "What I felt about it was.......")

For reviewing and appraisal (E16; "What was good/bad about that was.......")

In Guided Phantasies (G21: "When you walk through a door you will........")

28. BRIEFING NOTES AND HANDOUTS

Description

Means by which

a) Briefing and information can be given prior to a meeting so that people can come prepared for a discussion.

b) Information prepared in advance e.g. in the form of a summary, which can be taken away from a meeting. This possibly eliminates the need for note-taking, which can distract from the discussion.

c) Discussion can be focussed and developed during a meeting by members reading a selective piece or salient points prior to discussion.

d) Topics can also be presented by using visual aids. (See H).

Procedures

A. Briefing Notes: for information given in advance or during a meeting.

1. Prepare notes in advance; preferably have them typed.

2. Distribute to members in advance.

3. At the meeting allow time to read and check over for information and to make notes.

4. Seek agreements on points that may need (a) clarification; (b) elaboration; and (c) further and more detailed discussion.

Note: Always have spare copies available for those who (deliberately or otherwise) forget and have no notes.

B. Structured Reading: where the purpose and focus of the discussion is educational as opposed to business and problem solving, short articles can be used to introduce or reinforce key points.

1. Select material with care to ensure its relevance. Draw attention to key points by "glo lighting" the important sentences and paragraphs.

2. Follow the procedures outlined in A above for use during the meeting/session.

3. Where several articles are available on a subject or where the articles are long ones, separate reading tasks may be allocated to individual or sub groups, which report back their findings and conclusions to the total group. (See C7. Forming Sub-Groups)
For an example of this approach in practice see Part III (a)

4. Articles can be used to reinforce points missed in discussion or distributed after discussion.

Do's and Don'ts

— Notes/handouts may not be read if issued prior to the meeting, particularly too far in advance; a week is about the maximum.
You may need to allow time at the start of the session so that everyone starts from a similar knowledge base.

— To avoid people being distracted by reading matter during a discussion, always be clear when the handout is going to be used. State that time will be allowed for reading.

— Keep papers brief; only as much information as can be handled in the session. Otherwise people may feel overwhelmed and threatened or dominated by the material. Use the handout as a stimulus to discussion; to increase not inhibit participation.

When To Use

— To introduce a given agenda item during a meeting.

— To encourage discussion on a subject that is giving some concern e.g. the management of violent behaviour, drugs or solvent abuse.

29. PLANNING FRAMEWORKS

Description

These are tools to assist thinking about future actions and intentions. They can also be used to evaluate progress. Planning frameworks should be designed for specific purposes, and can take form of (a) questionnaires, (b) checklist or (c) pro-forma sheets.

a) Questionnaires — these are usually open-ended, requiring respondents to think about and record the details of their plans. These may, but do not necessarily, indicate the sequence in which plans are to be implemented. To do this an additional planning chart may be required.

b) Checklists — these are similar to the above, but act more as an aide memoire to ensure that certain tasks are carried out e.g.

— "What are the tasks, which have to be done today?"

— "To which should priority be given?"

— "Who are the people I need to see/contact?"

c) Pro-forma sheets — provide a more structured approach by using prepared headings and categories to guide thinking and planning. (See Personal Work Priorities example overleaf, also Action Planning G 22)

Objectives

1. To provide structured ways of planning activities.

2. To provide space to think things through before taking appropriate action.

3. To assist timetabling and the correct sequencing of events.

4. To assist with the ordering of future priorities.

5. To provide the basis for future evaluation of activities.

Procedures

1. Preparations

a) Consider the purpose for which a particular framework is needed before deciding on the particular format.

b) Choose a framework to meet that purpose. It is advisable to use the simplest method that will prove adequate for the purpose required.

c) Prepare the appropriate questions (for checklist/questionnaire) or headings if some kind of pro-forma is to be used. (Note: the attached are only examples - you may need to devise your own contents).

2. Implementation

Use the frameworks in conjunction with the appropriate methods/techniques described in Sections B and C (e.g. Nominal Group Technique, Sub Groups etc).

— Avoid having too many questions or headings, unless a considerable amount of detail is required and time is available to complete them.

— Usually more detailed information will be required for short-term planning e.g. "What are the tasks for the next week/month" longer term planning will tend to be expressed in more general terms, the details to follow later.

— When using a written questionaire or pro-forma ensure that there is sufficient space for written answers. This also applies if information is being recorded on large sheets for display.

— Encourage the planners to concentrate on recording key points only - avoid having too much detail.

— Ensure that these frameworks are used as tools i.e. to assist thinking, sharing of plans etc. not as ends in themselves.

When To Use

Examples

1. See also the Personal Disclosure Checklists in B 6 for some very simple planning frameworks.

2. See, for example, Action Planning (G 22) for an example of a planning framework and ideas for implementing change.

3. Two different kinds of planning frameworks are attached as further examples. One encourages people to think about their use of time and ordering of priorities; the other is to assist in work planning.

Example of Planning Framework 1.

PERSONAL WORK ASSESSMENT

STAGE 1

1. Think back day-by-day over the last 2 weeks and list the sort of activities in which you were engaged under the following 6 headings.

DIRECT CARE OF RESIDENTS OR USERS OF WORK CENTRE	STAFF DEVELOP- MENT & TRAINING	ORGANISING & PLANNING WORK TO MAINTAIN & DEVELOP SERVICES	WORK WITH CLIENTS' FAMILIES AND LOCAL COMMUNITY	LIAISON WITH REST OF AGENCY AND OTHER AGENCIES

2. a) Which activities took up most of your time?

  b) Which did you give very little time to?

3. a) What activities do you feel you give the right amount of time, energy and skill?

  b) What activities require a higher priority or more resources than they are given now?

STAGE 2

4. If you were able to change the way you use your time:

  a) What would you like to do more of?

  b) What do you feel you ought to do more of?

  c) What changes do you think you are likely to be able to make?

5. If you are to make some changes in your pattern of work:

  a) What will you need to cut out or spend less time on?

  b) What will you need to spend more time doing?

  c) Are there any things you do not do now but will need to start?

6. WORK CHANGE PLANNER

Note in the boxes any changes you plan to make in the next 6
months:

CHANGES	DIRECT CARE OF RESIDENTS OR USERS	STAFF DEVELOPMENT & TRAINING	ORGANISING AND PLANNING WORK TO MAINTAIN & DEVELOP SERVICES	WORK WITH CLIENTS' FAMILIES & LOCAL COMMUNITY	LIAISON WITH REST OF AGENCY & OTHER AGENCIES	OTHERS
ACTIVITIES TO CUT OUT OR SPEND LESS TIME ON						
ACTIVITIES REQUIRING MORE TIME						
NEW THINGS TO DO						

Example of Planning Framework 2.

**EXAMPLE OF INDIVIDUAL PLANNING DOCUMENT
FOR CHANGE STRATEGY**

STAGES OF DEVELOPMENT OF STRATEGY

	OPENING PHASE	INITIAL DEVELOPMENT PHASE	COMPETENT WORKING PHASE	CONSOLIDATION PHASE
EXAMPLES OF ACTIVITIES IN THESE PHASES ARE....				
WHAT I SHOULD DO IN EACH PHASE IS				
ACCEPTABLE OUTCOMES WOULD BE				
FAILURE WOULD BE INDICATED BY.....				
THE MAIN OBSTACLES I ANTICIPATE ARE....				

- Note: by activities we mean all the things you may become involved with, i.e. direct care, organising work, encouraging and motivating others and oneself, and working with other people.

30. LISTING AND CLUSTERING

Description

The "listing" and "clustering" refer to two related processes by which ideas and information are produced and sorted out into themes or categorised. Long lists of items are by themselves of limited value unless sorted out in some way. Clustering enables a large number of ideas to be reduced into fewer and more manageable catergories, which can then be used to focus further analysis and discussion.

Objectives

1. To record ideas or items of information as they are produced.

2. To reduce the material into more manageable categories by grouping related ideas.

3. To assist the setting of priorities for further work.

4. To assist analytical and problem-solving processes.

5. To focus on the salient issues or problems.

Procedures

A. Listing

Lists can be produced in several ways e.g. by brainstorming, calling out or by nominal group work. Usually a recorder is appointed or group members can write up their own statements themselves.

B. Clustering

Clustering, as does the production of lists, requires group involvement and decision making. Several methods can be used, viz:

1. Inspection method - take the first item on the list, look for others that are linked and mark off or re-write one under the other. Once that category is formed, take the next untreated item and repeat the process until the whole list has been categorised.

2. Nominal method - each person in the group writes down 2/3 themes, which are suggested to them. These are displayed and the group decides which items apply.

3. Round robin - one person identifies a possible theme and participants take turns to identify items from the list that reflect that theme.

Do's and Don'ts

— Items can often be eliminated, when they are clearly irrelevant.

— Sometimes a vote may have to be taken where agreement is needed over the inclusion of particular items and categories, or if priorities need to be established.

— If the original list is too long, the clustering too can become time consuming and loses its value.

— A clear focus needs to be maintained. Groups can easily be sidetracked into unproductive discussions on indivdual items or their categorisation. Discussion should come after a final list/cluster of items has been agreed.

When To Use

— Planning the equipping and use of a new play bus. The group is asked "All the things we need inside the bus are......" (then to list outside etc.)

— Listing out all the problems associated with a particular client/child/resident, which can be identified by different members of the group (a semi-brainstorming approach).

— Setting an agenda for a meeting by listing out all the possible items for discussion before sorting out in order of priority.

31. USING "PATTERN" RECORDING TECHNIQUES

Description

These are described by Buzan in "Use Your Head"[1] and provide an alternative or additional method for recording information and ideas to the more traditional linear note taking. Pattern note taking can be used by individuals or by groups using, for example, large sheets of paper or an overhead projector.

Advantages of pattern note taking are:

1. A set of related ideas can be taken in as a whole.

2. The connections and associations between ideas or sub themes can be demonstrated and registered.

3. It encourages new ideas and lateral thinking. As with many similar techniques once the basic principles are mastered individuals can develop their own variants and styles.

Objectives

1. To provide a creative approach to note taking and recording.

2. To encourage people to think in terms of "wholes" or "patterns" of ideas instead of a fixed sequence.

3. To encourage creativity and lateral thinking.

Procedures

The attached is an example of a pattern record from Buzan's book. The basic procedures to be followed are:

1. Start in the middle of a sheet of paper by identifying the theme or topic under consideration by writing it into a box, circle or 3-dimensional figure or even the "trunk" of a tree.

e.g.

2. From the "core" draw lines to represent "branches" of ideas. The branches usually identify key themes or sub-themes from which more specific ideas emerge and can be connected.

e.g.

3. Join up any related themes or ideas by means of arrows, dotted lines, different colours etc.

Do's and Don'ts

— When used as a recording or note-taking tool different branches or "twigs" can be added as the information is given (ideas are rarely presented or received in purely logical sequence).

— Be prepared to experiment and find your own style and variation.

When To Use

Examples:

— To collect ideas for a piece of project work.

— To summarise the salient details from a case record for a review or a case conference.

— To record a "brainstorming" exercise.

Notes and References

1. For further information about the theory of "patterns" and the techniques consult Buzan T. **Use Your Head.** London, BBC 1974.

Example of a pattern record.

ENDINGS

Emotional Reactions
- Excitement
  - Relief
  - Liberation
  - Enthusiasm
  - Hope
  - Optimism
- Loss
  - Anxiety
    - Fear
    - Despair
  - Depression

Ending Up Being A Student
- Breaking off Friendship
  - Loss of support

Looking To The Future
- Starting A New Job/Career
  - Reactions To Being A "New Person"
- New Friends And Relationships
- Returning To Be A Housewife or Husband
  - Being Unemployed

What Has Been Gained?
- Some Happy Times
- Knowledge Skills, Wisdom
- Lost Opportunities
  - Failing To Say What One Should
- Unhappy Moments
  - Regret At Saying Some Things

**PART III
EXAMPLES IN ACTION
(Set Menus)**

CONTENTS

This part of the guide shows a variety of methods and techniques in combination. All are taken from actual experience and attempt to cover a wide range of activities. In each case time was taken to plan both the content and processes of the event and care was taken to involve participants in the planning stages as well as the final events themselves. The spin-off effects from this kind of staff involvement is considerable in developing thier abilities both to use and improve these ideas in further activities. Our intention is not to encourage the user to copy these examples but to trigger ideas about how groups of methods and techniques can be used in practice.

Four examples are given:

a) A meeting called to obtain a group response to an agency working party document.   94

b) A day workshop to examine behaviour problems of children in a day nursery.   95

c) The use of sculpting techniques by an area team facing reorganisation.   97

d) A day workshop to review the structure of meetings in an area social services team.   98

a) A MEETING CALLED TO OBTAIN A GROUP RESPONSE TO AN AGENCY WORKING PARTY DOCUMENT

Description

Staff groups are often asked to comment on reports and documents of one sort or another. Such reports are often complicated, difficult to read and understand. Not surprisingly the information is often barely read or properly digested and its impact is lost. The objectives of this meeting called to examine a set of written proposals for changes to the organisational structure of the agency are:

1. For the staff group to read and understand the report with maximum participation and efficiency.

2. To reach an agreed response that is objective rather than emotional.

3. To ensure that the response made is a collective one i.e. "owned" by the whole group.

Planning and Participation

a) Prior to the meeting it is arranged for the report to be read by pairs of staff, each pair consisting of one senior and one junior member of the group.

b) Each pair is given the task of reading and reviewing one particular section of the report. The pairs are asked to record on large sheets of paper:

1. The main points covered in that section of the report

2. Any recommendations emerging from the section.

c) The sheets of paper are displayed in an "art gallery" for public viewing and informal disccussion prior to the meeting.

The Meeting

This goes through the following stages:

a) Questions for clarification and further explanation arising from the displayed material are listed and discussed.

b) A list of felt concerns and issues is made out. The issues are clustered under common headings and discussed. These are developed into statements forming the group's response to the general contents of the report.

c) Each recommendation in the document is then made subject to pieces of "good news/bad news" reported by the group. Those evaluations are also developed into statements which form the basis of the group's response to the report's recommedations.

Summary of Techniques Used (in alphabetical order)

1. Art Gallery (H 24)

2. "Good News/Bad News" (E 16)

3. Listing and Clustering (I 30)

4. Working in Pairs (C 7)

5. Structured Reading (I 28)

b) A DAY WORKSHOP TO EXAMINE BEHAVIOUR PROBLEMS OF CHILDREN IN A DAY NURSERY

Description

A day's workshop programme has been arranged for the staff of a day nursery to examine the problems raised by a small number of children, whose behaviour is causing concern. The stated objectives are:

— to provide an opportunity for staff to express their concerns and anxieties

— to get a perspective on these problems by examining their sources and effects

— to explore some alternative ways of managing the problems.

Planning

An interesting feature of this workshop is that the programme for the day is planned by the participants at the beginning of the workshop. The focus for the workshop has been identified beforehand but the contents are decided by the participants.

Preparations

These include:

— negotiating a date and times for the workshop;

— arranging a suitable venue to hold the workshop;

— making arrangements for staff on duty to be covered;

— obtaining a supply of large sheets of paper, felt tip pens, blue tac etc.;

— ensuring that there is a regular supply of coffee and light refreshments.

Process

Four stages can be identified in the running of the programme:

1. Identification of the problems

2. Assessment of the problems

3. Identification of ways of coping and managing the problems more effectively.

4. Review and evaluation.

(i) Identifying the problems

a) In this stage participants are asked to brainstorm problems and issues which they want to be tackled during the workshop. These are recorded on large sheets of paper.

b) The issues are then clustered into common themes and headings using a nominal approach. Each member is asked in turn to choose statements that imply a particular theme or main heading. Eight headings or themes are produced which are written up on another sheet of paper.

c) The rest of the brainstorm items are then allocated under the different headings by members choosing an item and ordering it under a particular heading. The process continues until all the items are dealt with.

d) The themes are translated into action statements which are put into an order of priority for consideration during the workshop. This list of topics becomes the programme for the day and a timetable is drawn up on this basis. The lists of items are then completed and placed side by side (see Fig 1. for an example).

Fig 1.

WHO ARE THE DIS-RUPTIVE CHILDREN	HOW ARE THEY DISRUPTIVE	HOW DO STAFF DEAL WITH DISRUPTIONS
John	Riot inciter, gets everyone over-excited, chaos, completely out of control.	Diversionary tactics Remove rioter from scene Turn riot into noisy play.

(ii) Assessment of the problems

a) This is done by the group carrying out a "good news/bad news" exercise on the identified issue. For example, under the heading "How do staff deal with disruptive behaviour?" a number of approaches can be identified. Each approach is to give a piece of "good news" and/or "bad news" as a way of evaluating its effectiveness (see Fig 2.).

Fig. 2

HOW DO STAFF DEAL WITH DISRUPTIONS	GOOD NEWS	BAD NEWS
Diversionary tactics	Child will often respond to diversion Can calm "rioter" giving other staff opporunity to settle rest of group.	Child getting used to tactic so less effective. Lots of staff energy needed to divert. Takes member of staff away from group activity. Stops disruption at time but does not prevent.
Remove rioter from scene	Always works Gives opportunity to talk to child. Encourages it to go back and rejoin group in a calm and co-operative manner etc.	Takes one member of staff out of group room, therfore puts more pressure on rest of staff Gives child individual attention in response to negative behaviour etc.

b) A further piece of assessment is to ask why do various problems arise? This question is tackled by another brainstorming exercise in which members throw out their theories and ideas.

(iii) Identifying ways of coping and managing the problems more effectively.

a) The first step is to assemble an art gallery of all the sheets of paper completed to date. This enables workshop members to make the links between the assessment of the problems and how they might reduce the problems.

b) The next step is to carry out another brainstorming exercise using the sentence "Some ways of coping are ..." as the trigger for ideas.

c) The results of this brainstorm are clustered, put into order of priority and used to devise an action programme in which group members are allocated specific tasks to complete, reading material is identified and an agreement to implement the plan is made.

(iv) Reviewing and evaluating the day

a) This is done using the nominal group approach. Each participant is asked to write down a response to the following:

"The important thing about today has been ...".

b) Answers are recorded on large sheets of paper and there is some discussion before dispersal.

Summary of Techniques (in alphabetical order)

1. Art Gallery (H 24)

2. Brainstoming (D 12)

3. Listing and Clustering (I 30)

4. Good News/Bad News (E 16)

5. Nominal Work Group (D 11)

6. Trigger Sentences (I 27)

c) THE USE OF SCULPTING TECHNIQUES BY AN AREA TEAM FACING REORGANISATION (See D 14)

Description

As part of a project involving an area social services staff group of about 20 workers, who are considering alternative models of organisation, one meeting is devoted to sculpting some different team structures. The purposes of the sculpts is to explore what it would feel like to belong to different types of team e.g. "generic" or "specialist" teams.

The total project lasts for about 3 months at the end of which decisions about proposed changes are taken. This exercise, which occurs in the early stages of the project, assists the evaluation of the various alternatives; this makes an important contribution to the final decision taking.

Many of the other techniques described in this manual are also used at different stages throughout the project, e.g. nominal group work, brainstorming, voting procedures.

Preparation

Each of the proposed posts or positions e.g. team leader, family aide, social worker, is written out in advance on a slip of paper and placed on a table.

The Session

a) Each participant is asked to select a slip of paper designating the position he/she wishes to occupy in the restructured office. (Inevitably some cannot get the post they seek).

b) The group is then briefed for the sculpting. There are to be 3 sculpts, the first two consisting of the alternative team models which have been suggested:

1. To reorganise into a number of smaller teams, each one specialising in a particular client group e.g. child care, elderly, physical handicap, mental health.

2. To develop small "patchwork" teams, each one being responsible for delivering the full range of services to a particular area.

c) In addition a third sculpt is done, which depicts how the whole area appears to relate currently from the point of view of the workers involved.

Results

a) The first two sculpts provide quite different configurations, the possible reasons for which are discussed fully afterwards. The sculpts also highlight cross boundary issues e.g. would "specialist" teams become too inward looking and isolated from the rest of the office? A similar problem emerges with the "patch" model, but it is felt there is greater commonality of interest and therefore flexibility. Another issue is: can elements of specialism be incorporated into a basic "patch" model, if so how? What would it feel like? (Note these issues can be explored further using more sculpting).

b) The third sculpt highlights problems in communication between management and practitioners. These issues too become the subject of further discussion, the use of sculpting having "broken the ice" as it were, allowing for the expression of feelings that might otherwise have remained unexpressed.

d) A DAY WORKSHOP TO REVIEW THE STRUCTURE OF MEETINGS IN AN AREA SOCIAL SERVICES TEAM

Description

A workshop has been organised for the members of a recently reorganised area social services office. The area now has two specialist teams, one dealing primarily with child care, the other with adult services work. Reorganisation from an essentially "generic" team structure has resulted in problems about which meetings are relevant for individuals to attend. There is a strong feeling amongst the total group that too much time is spent in meetings. Is this workshop going to reinforce those feelings?

The objectives of the workshop are established as:

1. To identify what meetings are the relevant ones for workers in either team to attend.

2. To decide on the structure and process of some of the meetings involving team members, i.e. who should meet with whom, about what, when and for how long.

Planning

a) The total group (at a preliminary meeting) delegates the planning and running of the workshop to a sub-group consisting of the two senior social workers and two basic grade workers nominated by the rest.

b) It is agreed that the planning group should draw up a provisional workshop programme, which would be amended (if necessary) before approval by the total group. It is also agreed that the programme should be sanctioned by line management as the outcomes might well result in proposals to change existing work practices. Any proposals would need to be ratified by the Area Director.

c) The Planning Group meets once a week on three occasions before the final progamme is drawn up and agreed by the total group.

Preparations

These include:

a) Deciding on the content of the programme and the methods to be used; for example, it is felt that outside speakers are not necessary and the group will need to retain its own resources and problem solving abilities.

b) Choosing a suitable venue, which needs to be comfortable and free from interruptions.

c) Considering the financial implications, including the costs of hiring a venue, arranging for tea and coffee, the typing up of a programme, the need for resources like large sheets of paper, felt tip pens etc.

d) Allocating tasks, e.g. who will be responsible for ensuring an ample supply of large sheets of paper and felt tip pens, who will introduce the day, who will explain the practical arrangements like where the toilets are to be found.

e) Choosing appropriate decision taking mechanisms since the objective of the day is to take decisions. It is agreed that a simple voting procedure should be used in the event of failure to reach a satisfactory concensus.

Process of the Workshop

The workshop follows a number of stages:

    Introductions

2. Evaluation of current arrangements

3. Development of alternative structures

4. Negotiation of a revised structure

5. Review and evaluation.

1. Introductions

    a) One member of the planning group takes responsibility for introducing the programme and the practical arrangements.

    b) Participants are then asked to do some nominal work (writing on their expectations and thoughts about the day ahead), which is then disclosed and recorded publicly.

2. Evaluation of current situation on "meetings"

    a) A "good news/bad news" exercise using the nominal group method is carried out in order to obtain a reasonably balanced view of the present position. Each individual writes out their statements, which are read out one at a time and recorded on large sheets of paper.

    b) These are then discussed in pairs and the product of the discussion fed back to the total group.

    c) A further nominal exercise is conducted to examine the purpose of meetings. The results are displayed as an "art gallery" which is viewed and discussed.

3. Development of alternative structures for meetings

    Each individual then tries to devise a new structure for meetings according to criteria that have been identified from the previous stages. Each set of ideas is recorded and displayed.

4. Negotiation stage

    a) Discussions take place about the most appropriate arrangements for group members. Voting procedures are not required as a concensus for a modified structure is reached.

    b) The new set of arrangements are written up and a plan for implementation drawn up.

5. Review and evaluation

    a) It is agreed that the process of the day has allowed maximum participation and the task objectives nave been reached.

    b) Agreement is also reached to review the new arrangements three months after implementation using a "good news/bad news" approach.

Summary of Techniques Used (in alphabetical order)

1. Art Gallery (H 24)

2. Forming Sub-Groups (C 7)

3. "Good News/Bad News" exercises (E 16)

4. Nominal Group Technique (D 11)

5. Trigger Techniques (I 27)

A Day Workshop To Review The Structure Of Meetings In An Area Social Services Team

PROGRAMME

9.30-9.45am   Coffee

9.45-9.55am   Start: individuals complete two cue (trigger) sentences on cards provided:
a) My main apprehension about today is.........

b) One positive thing I'm going to do to make today a success is........

Share in whole group and pin to the wall.

9.55-10.15am   Start main task

Objective — To work out what meetings are relevant for which workers to attend.

Outcome — To agree who meets with whom about what, when, and for how long.

10.15-10.30am   Introduction to the morning's process.

Coffee to be taken while working.

10.30-11.00am   In the whole group, the good and bad news about the present weekly team meeting is recorded; one good and one bad feature from each team member is taken in turn until all statements are recorded.

11.00-11.15am   Discuss in pairs the general reasons why a social services team needs to meet together in a group.

11.15-11.45am   Record feedback in the whole group

11.45-12.30am   Individual work on a large sheet of paper. Cue sentence:"The reasons I need to go to an office meeting/meetings in the area are......." When finished stick on the wall to form an "art gallery".

12.30-1.00pm   View the "art gallery" and discuss

1.00-2.00pm   Lunch

2.00-2.30pm   Individual work to create a structure which will include the above. The structure should include:

a) Who meets with whom

b) About what

c) Frequency

d) Open or closed

2.30-3.30pm   Directed feedback from each individual. A recorder is asked to summarise the proposals being presented.

3.30-3.45pm   Tea

3.45-4.30pm   Group discussion to negotiate a workable arrangement.

4.30-5.00pm   Write up the agreement, draw up a plan for implementation.

Review of the day before dispersal.